Castles in Colour

Castles

in Colour

Anthony Kemp

BLANDFORD PRESS
Poole

Line illustrations
Joyce Smith and David Dowland

Colour layout
Gordon Dowland

First published in 1977
by Blandford Press Ltd,
Link House, West Street,
Poole, Dorset BH15 1LL

Printed in Great Britain by W. S. Cowell, Ipswich
and Richard Clay (Chaucer Press) Bungay

CONTENTS

ACKNOWLEDGEMENTS

Colour transparencies for this book were especially selected from the work of the following photographers and from photographic archives as follows; *Belgian National Tourist Office*, jacket (rear), no. 19; *British Tourist Authority*, jacket (front), nos 51, 56; *John Burke, Esq.*, no. 21; *Czech National Tourist Office*, nos 25, 27, 69, 116; *Department of the Environment Photographic Library*, nos 7, 8, 12, 13, 15, 17, 40. 47, 48, 50, 52, 53, 57, 58, 64, 119; *French Government Tourist Office*, nos 44, 49, 117; *Clive Hicks, Esq.*, no. 67; *Dr. Quentin Hughes*, nos 3, 4, 10, 33, 41, 45, 77, 79, 91, 105, 110, 111, 114; *Italian State Tourist Office*, no. 115; *Michael Jarvis, Esq.*, nos 38, 54, 55, 65, 81, 82, 83, 84, 85, 86, 87, 89, 90; *Anthony Kemp, Esq.*, nos 2, 5, 9, 11, 36, 37, 39, 43, 46, 59, 63, 68, 104, 106, 107, 113; *Middle East Archive*, nos 22, 23, 24, 26; *A. H. Robson, Esq.*, no. 14; *Ronald Sheridan's Photo Library*, nos 1, 18, 20, 31, 32, 34, 35, 42, 70, 71, 72, 73, 74, 75, 76, 80, 112; *Tony Stone Associates*, nos 6, 16, 28, 29, 30, 78, 88, 92, 93, 94, 95, 96, 97, 98, 99, 100, 108, 120; *Swiss National Tourist Office*, no. 60; *Woodmansterne*, nos 61, 62, 66, 101, 102, 103, 109, 118, 121. *n.b.* no. 41 originally appeared in Hughes, J. Q., *Military Architecture*, Hugh Evelyn, London, 1974. Title page (Conisbrough Castle): *Department of the Environment Photographic Library*.

AUTHOR'S NOTE

The greatest debt of respect that an author owes, is to those who have gone before. Thus I must pay tribute to the numerous early chroniclers and more modern scholars whose labours have made this book possible. To Dr Quentin Hughes I am greatly indebted for much kindness and help. I must also mention Dr Paul Hyams, one of my tutors at Oxford. It was he who instilled into my often sceptical mind the knowledge I possess of mediaeval history. David Barnes undertook at short notice the onerous task of picture research. The illustrations are mainly the result of his application and initiative. Barry Gregory, of Blandford Press, gave me the opportunity to write this work. For this I am most grateful, as well as for his help and kindness in its preparation. Finally, there is my wife, who has been dragged around a great number of fortifications in Europe over the years. My thanks are due to her for her patience and understanding as well as her encouragement freely given for me to study.

INTRODUCTION

There is a vast amount of literature on the subject of castles, much of which is extremely specialized, especially from the architectural point of view. On the other hand there are books that present simply a selection of examples without any attempt to tie them together into a cohesive narrative. The aim here is to provide a general survey in the hope that it will stimulate the interest of the reader and be of help to those who like to visit castles. As there are so many, both ruined and intact, scattered all over Europe, only those castles important to the development of design features can be included. To those readers whose 'favourite' castle has been omitted, I offer my apologies.

By definition, a castle is the private stronghold of a feudal magnate, either baron or king. It is these elements of personal ownership and residence that characterize the pure mediaeval castle. In the ancient world fortifications were built which were under the control of the state or the particular community. The massive walls of the Greek cities and the camps of the Roman legions served the needs of the populace rather than the individual. The barbarian successors of the Roman Empire were not great builders and fought their battles in the open field. They in turn were followed by the Carolingian Empire which established once again a strong central government, whereby there was no need for the citizen to fortify his residence. Siege machinery was virtually unknown, and the weapons of attack and defence were limited to the hand thrown missile of various types. It was the collapse of this empire, the division of its territories into smaller units, and the pressure of Viking raids, that were to lead directly to the introduction of those buildings that we know of as castles.

The early castles were purely palisaded earthworks, designed to keep out lightly armed raiders and to provide a place of safety for the owner to store his goods. As weapons developed however, and the Romano-Greek siege engines were reintroduced, the need for stone protection became apparent. From the eleventh century onwards through the Middle Ages, castles became both stronger and more elaborate, but with a certain dichotomy becoming obvious. The original purpose as a place of refuge was being diluted by the desire for an increase in comfort, which led to the decline of emphasis on purely military design. In addition, states were becoming more powerful, and monarchs looked askance at their noble subjects entrenched in private strongholds. The final death-knell of the castle, together with certain social and economic changes, was the introduction of practical cannon, which rendered massive walls obsolete. Thus towards the end of the Middle Ages, the nobility tended to move into palace type residences, which however, often retained decorative defensive features. On the other hand, the state took over responsibility for national defence, and built artillery forts of purely military design with no sense of private ownership or residence.

In studying castles, one must not concentrate solely on their architecture, interesting though this is. They were part and parcel of mediaeval life, with an important rôle in warfare, government and the everyday activities of people of all classes. Consideration of these latter aspects may strip off some of the romantic allusions that still cling to them. To the humble peasant of the time, the castle was often a symbol of oppression and occupation by an alien power, far removed in spirit from the romanticism of such writers as Sir Walter Scott. To place the foregoing in perspective, let us attempt a twentieth century analogy, by imagining ourselves living in a small rural community somewhere in the civilised world at this moment in time. Let us then try to analyse our feelings if the following set of circumstances prevailed. All local government is concentrated in one fortified building on the edge of the village, and controlled by a hereditary lord, speaking perhaps a different language. His decisions would be absolute and enforced by a group of 'bully-boys', who could hunt at will over our carefully tended plots of land. We might be forced to labour for the lord and to provide him with goods and other services. Today we may exercise our democratic rights and complain about local government wastage, but in the Middle Ages, dissidents might well find themselves dangling from their lord's gallows!

A short bibliography has been included, listing works readily available through the Public Library system. The use of some technical words is unavoidable, and anyway, an understanding of these is an aid to the enjoyment of a visit to a castle. Those important technical words used in the text will be found in the glossary.

Anthony Kemp   East Preston, Sussex, 1977

I

FORTIFICATION IN
THE ANCIENT WORLD

Fortification can be defined as the creation of an obstacle between oneself and an enemy, or the improving of an already existing natural obstacle. The first military engineer was probably the cave-dweller who was faced with the problem of defending his lair against both wild beasts and his fellow-men. He solved this perhaps by barricading the entrance – high enough to discourage the would-be aggressor, and low enough to be able to see over the top and to throw missiles. Other primitive societies built their houses in trees, or on piles surrounded by water – all of them either creating an obstacle or improving a natural one. Another lesson soon learnt, was the advantage of height to the defender – it is easier to throw down a stone than to defy gravity by throwing it up. In addition, height confers the advantage of early-warning through observation.

In the Introduction, the castle was defined as a private stronghold, and as such was an element of fortification. Now everyone knows what a castle looks like, but before discussing the development of the mediaeval castle, we must try to place it in the general history of defensive architecture. The two basic elements of warfare are attack and defence and it is the advantage from time to time of one over the other that has governed all progress – from the day of the spear to the hydrogen bomb. The castle appeared at a time when defence was decidedly paramount. Weapons were primitive and their penetrating power was small, which meant that some sort of wall in most cases gave adequate protection. This factor was to remain constant until the advent of useful cannon at the beginning of the sixteenth century forced engineers to think again.

As mankind became more organised and began to settle down into fixed communities, defence became gradually more elaborate as earth walls were replaced by hewn stone. Some of the cities in Mesopotamia, the cradle of civilisation, were certainly surrounded by crenellated walls and had imposing towered gateways. The walls of Babylon were one of the Seven Wonders of the ancient world, and everyone knows that the walls of Jericho were apparently vulnerable to the music of a brass band. Reliefs found in Egyptian temples and dating from around 800 BC, show Assyrian walled cities together with such details as battering rams and undermining operations. The Egyptians themselves fortified many of their vast temple complexes with successive lines of walls becoming progressively higher towards the centre – foreshadowing the later concentric castle. Even earlier however, were the Greek fortresses of Mycenae and Tiryns which date from as far back as 1500 BC. Both these places show that the ancients understood the principle of making the approaches as tortuous as possible, and by introducing successive turns, forcing an attacker to expose his unshielded right side.

The Greeks were great fortifiers, and in the period from 400 BC to 200 BC, the art of war made great progress. At this time the principles of tension and torsion were first applied to the manufacture of siege artillery. Some of these ancient engines had a range of 500 metres (548 yds) and were extremely well constructed. Certainly Archimedes was a designer of such machines, and the active part he took in the defence of Syracuse in 215 BC is well chronicled. It was the Greeks who discovered the flanking tower which was to become one of the most important elements of future fortification. A plain wall can only be defended vertically, by dropping missiles or unpleasant substances on the attackers below, and to do this, the defenders have to expose themselves by leaning over. Adding projecting towers at intervals that correspond to the range of weapons in use, gives horizontal defence capability. From them, fire can be directed along the line of the wall as well as to the base. Additionally, by raising them higher than the intervening curtains, the wall-walk can be commanded as a defence against escalade, and to increase the range of any machines mounted on them.

The foregoing shows that most of the design features of the mediaeval castle were known to the ancient world, but all these works were essentially community projects. Although built as defences, they often tended towards the monumental, reflecting the power and the glory of the state that built them. Aristotle, in the *Politica*, while advocating the use of defences generally, says that 'the conclusion will be that the walls should always be kept in good order, and be made to satisfy both the claims of beauty and the needs of military utility.' This morale effect of fortification is often forgotten, but it had a great influence on the latter day development of the castle.

The Romans too were great military engineers, although the early Empire, being basically an aggressive organisation, had little use for permanent fortifications. Legions on the march in hostile territory however, threw up temporary earthworks to protect their camps. When it became necessary to base troops to hold down captured provinces, permanent forts were constructed. These were usually rectangular in shape, surrounded by a ditch and a wall flanked by towers. Inside, the buildings were laid out on a regular grid pattern with the main public buildings in the centre. The Roman towers were generally round or polygonal rather than square, as the angles of the latter were vulnerable to the attentions of battering rams. The Byzantines however, as the successors to the Roman tradition, reverted to the square form.

As the Roman Empire became larger, its frontiers extended to such a length that the available manpower could no longer adequately defend them. Thus the state found it necessary to fortify, especially in view of the growing pressure from encroaching barbarian tribes moving in from the east and the north. It is an old military adage that one man behind fixed defences is worth three men in the field, and by fortifying, one can hold a larger slice of territory with fewer men. The Romans tried to solve their problem with linear defences – individual forts conected by continuous stretches of ditch and rampart. This system had however, certain flaws. Firstly, only an extremely wealthy and well organised state could manage such vast projects. As an example, the *Limes Germanicus* ran from the Rhine near Koblenz to the Danube near Regensburg, a distance of some 300 miles, and were built early in the third century. The *Limes* consisted of isolated forts connected by walls, only part of which were stone. By far the greater length comprised earthen ramparts surmounted by wooden palisades and fronted by a ditch. The other example is of course, Hadrian's Wall, across the north of England. This came earlier than the *Limes*, having been built around 120 AD. The actual wall was some 73 miles long, and mostly followed the high ground that sloped steeply away in front. Sixteen main forts held the garrison, and every mile there was a smaller work in the form of a rectangular tower.

The second defect of this type of defence was that the attacker could choose the time and place of his attack – which meant that the whole length of the line had to be permanently and equally strongly garrisoned. Once an attack had commenced, the threatened sector had to be swiftly reinforced with reserves, thus denuding another area. The Romans however, had not really understood the idea of defence in depth, and failed to build strongpoints behind their lines. Once an invader was through, he could easily devastate the country behind, besides which, once such a line was outflanked, it became useless. The French found this out in 1940 when the Maginot Line was forced to surrender to an enemy who was already at the back door.

The problems of barbarian invasion and internal troubles also persuaded the Romans to turn their attention to fortifying their cities. A powerful central government has little need for fixed defences, but where anarchy reigns, it is up to each individual or community to look to their own security. This very lack of centralized power during the early Middle Ages, led to the proliferation of castles, but as the nation states grew slowly in influence, so the number of castles decreased.

Roman fortifications were a continuation of the Greek tradition, refined through experience and quality of workmanship. The last examples of Roman work in Britain can be seen in the remains of the so-called forts of the Saxon Shore. Nine of these were built along the coast between Norfolk and Hampshire to repel the raids of Saxon pirates, towards the end of the third century AD. All of them were based on the normal grid pattern and rectangular in shape, except for Pevensey which had an oval enceinte. There are extensive remains of several of them, and Norman castles were constructed within the forts at Portchester and Pevensey. The latter has Roman walls some 4 metres (13.1566 ft) thick, flanked by semi-circular towers. The two gateways were flanked by drum towers on both sides, a favourite Roman design that was later to become standard again in Europe generally. The sheer size of the fort can only be judged when one views the Norman castle tucked away in one corner, almost like an afterthought, the masonry of which has not survived as well as the original. Pevensey is an interesting example of the continuity of defence on a particular site. Within the complex are the remains of a Tudor artillery battery, while cunningly concealed among the ruins are a number of 1940 'pill-box type' bunkers.

The fall of the Roman Empire in the west brought with it a decline in the art of fortification. At first the barbarian invaders were on the move, and even when they finally settled, they preferred to fight in the open field. They were not basically city dwellers, and allowed the Roman city walls to decay – an exception being the Visigoths who built the original defences of Carcassonne. In the east however, the Empire continued under the rule of the Byzantine emperors, who inherited the tradition of building permanent defences. It was not until the start of the Crusading movement at the end of the eleventh century, that East and West were once again to come into military contact with one another. Most of the important stages in the development of the castle came after this. Those who went to the east saw examples of Byzantine and Arab work, and at the same time, Roman treatises on fortification became once more available. In these could be found exact details of siege machinery and chapters on basic design features. The old methods had never entirely died out in the west, but it is undoubtedly true that the experiences of the Crusaders had an enormous influence on the castle as a whole. In fact, most of the history of mediaeval defence is one of re-discovery rather than of innovation.

2

ON CASTLES IN GENERAL

This short chapter contains a certain amount of theory, but before the reader becomes impatient, let me hasten to add that there is a reason for this. Certain general principles applied to castles at all stages of their development, and a proper understanding of these is necessary for a thorough grasp of the subject. We have determined that a castle had an element of proprietorship about it, and in fact, the owner could be a king or emperor, a bishop, a great nobleman or a simple knight. Thus it could serve a greater national purpose or purely parochial ends.

To the casual observer today, it may seem that the ruins scattered romantically over the landscape and often far from the beaten track, must have been built largely at random. This may have been true in a few cases, but their owners, by and large, were experienced military officers - who would not have spent large sums of money for no good purpose. The very ability to build a castle was tied to the available finance, and the resources of the potential enemy.

In the early Middle Ages, vast areas of Europe were covered by forests, which could only be crossed by a few established tracks. The main routes followed the river valleys, except where the Roman roads that remained ignored the contours. Here of course is the reason for the proliferation of castles along such valleys as the Rhine and the lower Seine. Many of these ancient routes however, are no longer in use, and often only the works built to overlook them can be seen today.

The siting of a defensive work, whether it was a castle or a nineteenth century fort has not really changed. The following is a list of sites recommended for fortification and compiled in 1898 by an officer in the Royal Engineers:

'Centres of national, industrial or military importance.
Places which may serve as bases for field armies.
Important cross-roads.

Bridges (fords) over important rivers.
Lines of communication across frontiers.
Mountain passes.'

All of these factors could equally apply to the mediaeval castle. As an example, the ruins of Wallingford castle are situated at the edge of one of the many small towns along the Thames valley. As the name implies however, in former times there was a ford there, one of the most important crossing places between London and Oxford. William the Conqueror crossed at Wallingford on his way from Hastings to the final surrender of the Anglo-Saxons at Berkhampstead.

The castle appeared in Europe in the ninth century, as a direct result of Norse raids on the coast of present day France. These early structures fulfilled a purely defensive rôle which the state itself was unable to exercise. The siting of them was purely tactical, as they sprang up wherever there was a need, and in the absence of any overall defensive policy. By delegating authority for defence however, great power was delivered into the hands of the owner of a castle – a power that was often to be used for the benefit of the individual rather than that of the community as a whole. This led directly to the growth of the feudal system in Western Europe, a subject about which much has been written. Basically, it was a form of social and political organisation whereby a monarch made grants of land in return for specific services, mostly of a military nature. Society thus became a form of pyramid with the monarch at the top who lived from his own lands or demesne. The rest of his territory was granted to tenants-in-chief in return for the services of specific numbers of knights. In order to fulfil this obligation, the tenant-in-chief granted feoffs or parcels of land to lesser nobles and knights. The church also held land in return for knight service. The vast rural proletariat was made up of serfs bound to the land and required to labour for their lord, with the addition of a certain number of freemen of the yeoman class. The agreement however, was not totally one-sided. A lord was obliged to protect his tenants, and in times of unrest, the castle could become a place of refuge for the rural population. Anybody who wishes to understand the feudal system in operation cannot do better than read the book *William Marshall* by Sidney Painter – the story of one of the foremost knights of Western Europe.

On a purely parochial scale, the castle of a petty lord exerted influence over an area of land to the extent which could be patrolled by mounted men. It could also be used as a base for exactions of various kinds, such as customs dues and bridge tolls. On the positive side, the castle was often the centre of local government and justice in a period when the state could not fulfil this responsibility. Without this delegation, backed up by a certain amount of force, the anarchy might have been worse, and as a result, a comparatively large number of men gained experience in administration. As states became better organised however, castles were a hindrance to the establishment of royal power, but were troublesome to reduce.

On a larger scale, the castle system developed into a form of defence in depth, especially where the individual castles along a frontier were close enough together to be mutually supporting. It is often written that such and such a castle 'commanded' a certain feature. This was only true so long as that castle was not opposed by sufficient numbers to surround and neutralize it. If the path of an invading army was strewn by castles, that army had either to detach sufficient numbers to mask each one, or to actively besiege them, for any castle left untaken in its rear could easily disturb the communications of the invader. Now the mediaeval army was usually little better than an armed horde, which under the terms of feudal service, could seldom be kept in the field for more than 40 days. In addition, in a world dominated by agriculture, armies had a habit of melting away at harvest and seed time. Mercenary armies were unreliable and expensive, and their upkeep was within the means only of powerful monarchs. Thus well sited castles covering a frontier for example, could so delay an enemy that either his army would break up of its own accord, or time would be squandered in futile sieges.

The foregoing applies to castles in terms of grand strategy, but it is probable that in the early years, such strategic thinking was accidental. There were no maps on which a commander could plan the siting of his defences. He would, however, try to grant lands on a vulnerable frontier to powerful and loyal vassals, especially when the possible lines of approach were limited. At the end of the thirteenth century, Edward I set out to conquer Wales once and for all, and in his subsequent castle building programme, we see the beginnings of clear strategic thinking, as opposed to immediate tactical necessity.

The castle fulfilled not only a purely defensive rôle. In many cases, castles were built to hold down captured territory and to administer it. In times of war, they could act as a secure base for wide-ranging operations, and to secure lines of communication. In addition, their garrisons could undertake offensive sorties into neighbouring areas, to destroy crops for example. This is one reason for the surprisingly large number of mounted men usually found in a garrison.

As we look at the international development of the castle, one feature that will become readily apparent is that design details were often common to several countries. It must be remembered in this connexion that the European nobility formed an international caste, whose members had more in common with each other than with the peasants on their lands – who often spoke a different language. In the early Middle Ages there was little conception of nationhood, and a man's loyalties were to his lord rather than to the abstract idea of country or race. A knight from southern England would have been far more at home in France than in Northumberland. The Crusades also furthered this sense of an all-nation brotherhood of arms, as did the supranational scope of the Church.

Castles are often described as being impregnable, but there was really no such thing. Certain of them were very well built and strongly sited, so that they were difficult to attack. Others were never put to the test as their nuisance value was perhaps not considered great enough. All however, would eventually succumb to starvation. There were various factors that determined the resistance of a castle to a siege, which can be summarized as follows:

A successful creation of an obstacle and adaptation to the environment.
Sufficient supplies and water.
The morale of the commander and his garrison.

If all the above factors were present, and a vigorous defence was prosecuted, there was always the problem of treachery. It often made sense to change to the winning side or to accept a bribe. Indeed, if the garrison prolonged their defence unreasonably, they could expect to be put to the sword when the place eventually capitulated!

Following on these general thoughts, we will now examine the development of the mediaeval castle in Europe from its primitive beginnings to its decline into magnificent antiquity.

3
FORTIFICATION IN EUROPE BEFORE 1100

The collapse of the Roman Empire in the fifth century brought chaos to Europe, a situation that was only stabilized under the powerful personal rule of Charlemagne. The Carolingian Empire was an aggressive organisation, largely occupied in bringing Christianity to the East – by means of the sword if necessary. It had no real need of internal defences, although defended camps and townships were established in the newly-won territories.

In England, after the departure of the legions, the Romano-British population retreated westwards in the face of Germanic invaders from the continent, often seeking temporary refuge in the Iron-Age hill forts that still dotted the landscape of southern England. After the Saxons came the Danes, and under Alfred and his successors in their attempts to reunite the country, a system of defended townships grew up. These were known as burghs, but their defences were simply earthworks topped by palisades – at the most, the vulnerable gateway would have been stiffened by a wooden strongpoint. The early English kings were able to establish a strong enough central monarchy so that a feudal type of society failed to develop. The only castles to be built in England around that time were one or two constructed in the middle of the eleventh century by Norman followers of Edward the Confessor, and which are mentioned in the *Anglo-Saxon Chronicle*. Two of these were in Herefordshire, Ewyas Harold and Richard's Castle. Although built to keep the Welsh tribes in check, their lords so oppressed the local people that there was a popular uprising. Richard's Castle is situated overlooking Ludlow, and consists of a mound some 20 metres (66 ft) high and surrounded by a ditch. It was this very lack of castles in England that made the Norman conquest possible, according to the early historian Orderic Vitalis.

The Germanic word burgh originally meant a protective enclosure, but became transferred to the object protected. It remains as the English word borough, and as burg, the German name for a castle. In fact, the English did not have such a word to describe something that they knew nothing about. Orderic Vitalis says that the French called castles *castella* which in turn was borrowed from the Latin for a camp. Thus *The Oxford Dictionary* confirms that our word castle comes from Old Northern French.

In France however, the story was rather different, and explains why Edward's imported Normans promptly built castles. The splitting up of the Carolingian Empire led to a decline in the power of the central government – a decline that became most apparent under the threat of Viking raids. At first, local magnates were encouraged to build strongholds to defend their territories from the pirates, but in 864, the king, Charles the Bald, forbade further construction. His subjects were becoming too independent. The prohibition did not last long however, as the administration could not cope with the problem without the support of the nobility. A prayer spoken in the churches at the time was – *a furore Normannorum, libera nos Domine.* The Normans or Northmen who were the subject of this prayer were not in fact French, but Scandinavian pirates. One of them, however, Rollo, was given a grant of land by the French king, and it was he who went on to found the dynasty of the Dukes of Normandy. It was this hardy race that was to have such an influence on castle building and architecture generally, as well as the course of English history.

The typical Norman stronghold was of the type that we know as the motte and bailey castle. The word motte has nothing to do with the modern term moat. It was simply a natural or artificial mound, used for the purpose of gaining height. It was surrounded by a ditch, the spoil from which was used in building up the motte. This was crowned by a wooden palisade, within which the owner built his tower – also of wood. According to the rather stylistic designs of the Bayeux Tapestry, our only pictorial evidence for early castles, some of the towers were built on stilts, while the motte itself was built of layers of different materials.

The mound was connected to the bailey by a sloping bridge. All that the bailey consisted of was a simple courtyard enclosed by an earth rampart and palisade, outside which was a ditch – wet or dry. As space on top of the motte was strictly limited, the bailey housed the stables and other domestic buildings necessary for the maintenance of the castle and its garrison. The entrance was over the ditch via some form of removable

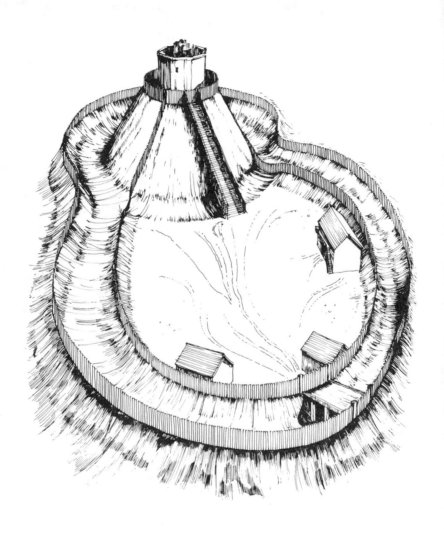

Fig. 1   An artist's reconstruction of a motte and bailey castle.

bridge.

The normal pattern was for the motte to be built on one side of the bailey, giving the castle the appearance of a figure-of-eight shape. The reason for this is often stated that it was to allow the garrison to escape once it had retreated into the tower. This however, is unlikely, as it would be extremely hazardous to scramble down the steep side of the motte and across the ditch under hostile fire. And anyway, not all castles had the motte at the edge. Bramber, in Sussex, featured the mound in the middle of an oblong bailey, while Windsor Castle's mound stood in the centre between two baileys, a layout similar to that of Arundel; Lewes had two mottes, quite some distance from each other.

This early form of castle appears all over western Europe, but mainly in England and France. If the tower was the basic element of defence until the end of the fifteenth century, the motte and bailey castle was a variation particularly suited to non-mountainous areas without ready supplies of stone. It was cheap and simple to build, and difficult to capture, as siege artillery was relatively unknown at the time. It also removed the advantage of the mounted knight over the foot soldier. It had however, certain inherent disadvantages. It was extremely vulnerable to fire, and cannot really have been conceived with lengthy resistance in mind – the problem being that it was difficult to organise any form of water supply on top of an artificial mound.

Parallel to the motte and bailey castle, another type developed in France as far back as the tenth century. This was the rectangular stone donjon or keep, usually associated first with the Normans in England after 1066. The idea did not stem from the motte and bailey, but was simply another solution to the problem of gaining height. The earliest of these castles was probably the one at Langeais, built somewhere around 990 by Fulk Nerra, Count of Anjou. Together with the contemporary castles of Montbazon and Montrichard, both of similar type, it secured one of the valleys leading to Tours on the Loire. Langeais, of which only the first two floors remain, measured 17 metres (56 ft) by 8 metres (26 ft) on the ground. There was no internal vaulting or stone staircases, and the strip buttresses were probably added later. Like most other keeps of the type, the entrance was on the first floor, the ground floor being used purely for storage purposes. Montbazon was some 30 metres (98.4 ft) high and had three floors above ground level.

The most impressive of these early stone donjons is undoubtedly

Loches, a short distance southeast of Tours on the Loire, and also actually a part of the strategic system around that city. It was built in the early part of the eleventh century and still stands to the magnificent height of 38 metres (125 ft). Its walls were 3 metres (10 ft) thick, and again, the entrance was on the first floor via a forebuilding or small keep.

The rarity of stone donjons at this time can be accounted for by their cost to erect and the need for skilled tradesmen to construct them. Such mighty piles of masonry testified to the prestige of their owners, but could only be defended passively. By making the entrance narrow and difficult of access, they could not be used by the garrison for swift sorties. Thus they were only 'bolt-holes' for use after the bailey had fallen. In view of the fact however, that at the time they were conceived, the long-service mercenary army had not been available, they could stand a limited siege with impunity. Of the five castles shown on the Bayeux Tapestry, only one, unidentified, is of stone.

As every schoolboy knows, in 1066, Duke William of Normandy came to England, and after winning the Battle of Hastings, which was not at Hastings, conquered the country. For the Duke and his followers, most of whom were there for the loot, England in defeat represented the legitimate spoils of war. The Anglo-Saxons who had largely lived at peace with their neighbours without the need for fortifications, were reduced to the status of a subject population, and the country was divided up among the Normans on a feudal basis. To hark back however, to the mechanics of the Conquest, one of William's first actions was to fortify his base camp – by building a castle at Hastings of the motte type. One account says that he brought this over with him in pieces – the instant prefabricated castle. As he had landed originally at Pevensey, he would have been confronted with the massive Roman walls of the fort there, with its prominent flanking towers, and it is strange that this idea was not re-employed as a consequence in England until over a century later.

Throughout the length and breadth of the country, the new masters arrived to take up their share of the loot, and wherever they found themselves they built their castles – over a hundred motte and bailey types were constructed prior to the year 1100. Not all of them belonged to noblemen however, for William reserved a large share of the land for himself which also had to be secured by castles. It is interesting to note that these royal foundations were often sited on the edge of existing towns with a view to dominating a potentially rebellious population. In other cases where a castle was built to dominate a strategic point, a township tended to grow up around it to administer to its needs.

The distribution of lands was probably done on a haphazard basis. William did not have the benefit of Ordnance Survey maps. Most of his followers received their feoffs made up of parcels in several counties – perhaps to hinder the build-up of cohesive principalities that could threaten royal control. An exception to this was in the areas along the Welsh border – the Marches – where it was necessary for the barons to have compact holdings in view of the state of almost continual warfare. Among the first castles to be built in England after the conquest were those along the south coast – Pevensey, Lewes, Bramber and Arundel. Then the Thames valley was fortified at Windsor, Wallingford and Oxford. (Of the latter, only the motte and part of a tower remains.) Berkhampstead, where the remaining Anglo-Saxons finally submitted to William, was also probably one of the first. As the later masonry has almost all disappeared, one can see there very clearly the original shape of the bailey with its motte at one corner. As the new king extended his power, so did the territory controlled by castles increase.

Beside the mass of motte and bailey castles, two stone keeps were built during the reign of William I. The best known of these is of course the White Tower, still the centrepiece of the Tower of London. The name is indicative of the fact that castles were often painted, and were not necessarily the grim ivy-clad ruins that we see today. The construction of the Tower was supervised by Gundulf, Bishop of Rochester, on a design similar to the earlier Angevin keeps. It was not however an exact rectangle, as the apse of the chapel protruded on one face. The entrance was above ground level via the usual fore-building, and the inside was divided into two by a strong partition wall. The strip buttresses at the corners were continued above the roof level to form small turrets. The other early stone keep was at Colchester, built probably as a counter to continuing Viking raids. It also featured a projecting chapel apse, but there only the first two storeys are intact with the remains of a third.

In discussing keeps it is important to remember that they were the owner's residence as well as the fighting platform. The same applied to the towers on top of mottes. On account of their essentially temporary nature, there is no such thing as a fully intact motte and bailey castle that can be visited. Only their remains are scattered all over the country, and many were later incorported into stone-built castles. We have however

Chapel

Inner Bailey

Keep

Outer Bailey

Hall

Barbican

Fig. 2   Plan of a mediaeval castle showing curtain walls, bailey and keep.

various descriptions of them left to us by the chroniclers. Jean de Colmieu described the castle at Merchem in Flanders as follows – 'It is the custom with the wealthy men and nobles of this area, because they spend their time in enmity and slaughter, and in order that they may be safer from their foes, and by their superior power either conquer their equals or oppress their inferiors, to pile up a mound of earth as high as they can, and to dig around it a ditch of some breadth and great depth, and, instead of a wall, to fortify the topmost edge of the mount round about with a rampart very strongly compacted of baulks of timber, . . . Within the rampart they build in the midst a house or citadel dominating the whole site.' Lambert of Ardres is more specific about the interior domestic arrangements in describing the great wooden tower house built around 1099 at Ardres in the Pas de Calais. 'The first storey was on the ground level where there were cellars and granaries and great boxes, barrels, casks and other household equipment. In the storey above were the dwelling and common rooms of the residents, including the larders and buttery, and the great chamber in which the lord and his lady slept. Adjoining this was . . . the dormitory of the ladies-in-waiting and the children. In the upper storey of the house were attic rooms in which on one side the sons of the lord, when they so desired, and on the other side the daughters, because they were obliged, were accustomed to sleep. In this storey also the watchmen and the servants appointed to keep the house slept at various times. High up on the east side of the house, in a convenient place, was the chapel. . . . There were stairs and passages from floor to floor, from the house into the separate kitchen . . . and from the house into the gallery where they were wont to entertain themselves with conversation . . .' This description conveys a certain regard for comfort, and certainly an awareness of the need for privacy for the women and children. It cannot be regarded though as being typical.

Towards the end of this period, with the Normans becoming established in England, tentative steps were already being taken to replace wooden castles with more durable constructions in stone. In addition, on rocky sites where this material was readily available, stone was used from the beginning. Richmond castle in Yorkshire has extensive remains of an eleventh century curtain wall, although the great keep is of a later date. Ludlow was also built on a rocky peninsula without motte or keep. Thus it was logical to surround the place with a stone wall rather than a wooden palisade, and to defend the entrance with a stone gatehouse – which was later converted into a keep by blocking up the doorway. Ludlow is also interesting in that it represents a first hesitant use of flanking towers in England since Roman times, and was almost certainly built before 1200. The towers were rectangular and were not well enough spaced to have been able to flank the whole enceinte, but their existence proves that there must have been some awareness of the need for horizontal defence, at this early date.

In France, apart from the example of the donjons already mentioned, there was little stone building in the eleventh century. The Normans however, had not only conquered England; they had also spread to Italy where their first centre of power was Salerno; the fortress of Aderno was built by Roger I who died in 1101 and this was a pure Norman rectangular keep with an internal division similar to that of the White Tower. Originally however, it was built without supports – the present chemise with corner buttresses is later in date. In the rest of Italy, it was the basic idea of the tower that dominated defensive thinking. Such towers had originated as a counter to Saracen raids along the coast, but in the eleventh century began to appear in the towns.

In Germany, the feudal system, and with it the private stronghold developed later than in France and England. The early castles were based on the tower, not as a residence, but as a place of refuge. Thus they were much taller and slimmer than their Norman counterparts, and were surrounded by a wall within which were the domestic buildings. The actual living area was a hall which in many cases was directly connected to the tower by some form of drawbridge. The two castles at Ruedesheim on the Rhine are examples of this type. Both consisted of a rectangular tower inside a surrounding curtain wall, and date from the middle of the eleventh century. In southern Germany, Switzerland and Austria however, there are certain towers that were built primarily as residences. An example is the original seat of the Habsburg family in Switzerland, built around 1020. Yet another variety is the *Wallburg*, entirely without tower and relying solely on a curtain. It is this very proliferation of styles in the Germanic countries, which makes intelligent classification so difficult.

Private strongholds had become firmly established in certain parts of Europe, coupled with the feudal system of land tenure. Both in France and England, defensive buildings had also to provide a satisfactory standard of accommodation for the owner and his retainers and family. Whatever romantic notions one may have about castles, the fact remains that to the bulk of the populations, they were symbols of oppression, often ruled by brutalized and unscrupulous lords.

4

THE TWELFTH
CENTURY CASTLE

There were two external factors, one immediate and the other becoming apparent towards the end, that had an influence on castle design during this century. The first was the Crusading movement which began with the inauguration of the First Crusade in 1096. The second was the courtly love movement which started in Provence during the latter part of the century. This was to do much towards reducing the brutality of the knightly classes by turning their minds away from slaughter for the sake of it, to romance. It is in the poems of this period that the nineteenth century romantic view of the castle found its inspiration – the songs of minstrels, damsels in distress and the widespread slaying of dragons and ogres. Chaucer's knight was not a brutal robber: he loved truth and honour, freedom and courtesy; he was a 'verray parfit gentil knight'.

Much has been written about the influence of the Crusades on western military architecture, but it is difficult to be definite about this. The absence of written records leaves us in the realms of supposition. It is a fact however, that the Crusaders right from the start came into contact with fortifications undreamed of in the West. The Byzantine Empire had continued and refined the Roman tradition without a break or an intervening Dark Age. One of the first sights that confronted the participants on the First Crusade when they arrived at Constantinople, was the Theodosian Wall. This had been built by the Emperor of that name at the beginning of the fifth century to guard the landward side of the city. The inspiration for the later concentric castles in Palestine and Western Europe has often been attributed to this wall, most of which still remains. It opposed successive lines of defence to the attacker. First came a ditch, with a terrace or list between it and the outer wall, flanked at regular intervals by rectangular towers. Then came another narrow terrace, and the inner wall, some 5 metres (16.4 ft) thick at the base – this was also flanked and being higher, commanded the lower defence levels. The list between the two walls formed a sort of 'killing-area' – a confined space where an attacking force would be bereft of cover and room to manoeuvre – and subject to a shower of missiles from the walls and towers above. By way of contrast, the walls of Rome were only single, although massive.

Following their stay at Constantinople, the Crusaders moved off into Asia Minor, which was hostile country, and came to a halt at Nicaea, which they decided to besiege. This was a large town entirely surrounded by a double girdle of walls and flanking towers, which had probably been built originally by Justinian in the fifth century. Certainly a hard nut to crack for a western army in 1097 when we consider the state of fortification described in the previous chapter. Anna Comnena however, a contemporary Byzantine historian, tells us about Raymond of Toulouse building a siege tower and employing miners. She also tells us that he had siege engines ready to batter the walls. It has often been assumed that such methods were rediscovered as a result of the contact with the east at the time of the Crusades, but the foregoing proves that there must at least have been an awareness of such engineering among the western commanders. It is safe to assume however, that the experiences of the Crusaders and the knowledge they gained were put to practical use when they returned home.

After Nicaea, the Crusaders moved south with great difficulty until they came to Antioch, another Roman walled city, which they managed only to capture by dint of treachery from within. Finally, in 1099, they took Jerusalem, and celebrated by butchering the population – blood ran ankle deep in the streets according to one account. For most of the Crusaders, that ended the matter as they had fulfilled their vows. Many of them returned home, leaving only a third of their number in Palestine faced by both a hostile population and environment. The European upper class in Palestine never numbered more than a few hundreds; they solved matters according to their own ideas by introducing the feudal system into their newly created principalities. Faced with the problem of having too much territory to be controlled by too few men, they built castles. These works, among the most interesting ever built, will be discussed at a later stage.

Not all Byzantine military architecture was antique Roman, however. Although most of their works featured the rectangular tower, they were apparently aware of the virtues of the round shape – advocated as far back as 30 BC by the writer Vitruvius. He pointed out that square shapes could have their angles easily broken by battering rams and miners' picks.

Additionally, a round tower could be vaulted internally, thus adding to its strength, and needed less masonry for a given area. Twin strongholds were built on either side of the Bosporus in about the year 1100 by Emperor Alexis Comnenus – some 7 miles north of Constantinople. Part of one of these is the massive Black Tower at Roumeli Hissar, 26 metres (85 ft) in diameter and rising through seven storeys to a height of 37.5 metres (123 ft) – the upper two levels having been added in the fifteenth century by the Turkish conquerors. In the middle of the twelfth century, two further castles featuring round towers were built on the Bosporus – Roumeli Kavak and Anadoli Kavak.

Returning for the moment to the West, we find castle building continuing along the old established lines of the motte and bailey and the keep and bailey. An important innovation though, was the shell keep that made its appearance at the beginning of the century. Its development was entirely logical, and it did not in any way supersede the rectangular keep, as has been suggested by some writers. The owner of a motte and bailey castle, faced with the problems of timber preservation in a damp climate, found that the answer was to replace his palisade with a stone wall. Even if his finances had run to a rectangular stone keep, he would have had difficulty in building it on the weak foundation of an artificial mound anyway.

There are many examples of shell keeps of both round and polygonal form. They were sometimes built round the base of the motte, sometimes around the middle and sometimes directly at the top. The best known is perhaps at Restormel in Cornwall, still remarkably well preserved. It has not lost its identity in a mixture of later building that has been superimposed on so many other castles. Restormel was circular with the wall-walk some 8.5 metres (28 ft) above the courtyard, which was simply formed by flattening the top of the motte. Within the outer shell was an inner wall, and between the two, a range of rooms and chambers. A towered gateway breaks the circle, and almost opposite this there is a projecting chapel added in the late thirteenth century. At Arundel, a riot of nineteenth century imaginary reconstruction, the shell keep is about all that remains of the original work. The shell built by Henry I on the motte at Windsor received its present shape complete with machicolation at the hands of Wyattville also in the nineteenth century. Other examples in the West country are at Totnes and Launceston. The logical successor to the shell-keep was of course the walled bailey. In many cases

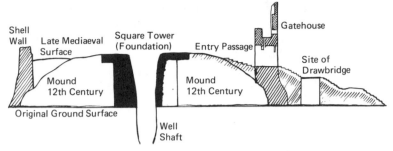

Fig. 3   Cross-section of Farnham Castle.

the palisade was replaced at roughly the same time with a wall of stone which was carried up the sides of the motte to join on to the keep.

One of the most interesting examples, and one that is worth more detailed examination is Farnham Castle in Surrey. This was built by Henry of Blois, Bishop of Winchester in around 1138, and started life as an artificial motte with, of all things, a stone tower on top. The problem of foundations was solved by carrying the walls down inside the mound to the original ground level and splaying them out on top to gain a sufficiently large building platform. The water problem already alluded to as far as artificial mounds were concerned, could thus be solved by digging a well shaft at the bottom of the foundations. The worthy bishop however, got on the wrong side of Henry II, and in 1155 his castles were slighted, including the tower at Farnham. It is not clear who built the present shell keep, but it was probably at the end of the twelfth or the beginning of the thirteenth century. Whoever it was had available a mound with the wreckage of the tower on top. They solved the problem by building a wall around the base of the mound, fitted with small rectangular flanking towers. Inside, the motte was levelled and the gaps around the edge filled to form a fighting platform. Except for the gatehouse, there was no living accommodation in the keep, and the domestic buildings would have been in the bailey. It is worth pointing out at this stage that flanking towers on a curved surface are rather pointless, as there is always a patch of dead ground between each pair.

In discussing castles in England, one must bear in mind that they were not a product at this time of native ingenuity – they were built by Norman Frenchmen. Probably the only English contribution lay in wielding a shovel as part of a forced labour squad. The kings during this century were foreigners, far more interested in their continental possessions and using England as a source of finance to pay for mercenary armies. The much beloved Richard I, the Lion-Heart, in fact, spent only 5 months of his 9 years reign in England. His father, Henry II, achieved stability and established financial and legal reforms, in order to be able to wage war in France without worrying about his rear. Stone construction of castles was still very much the exception rather than the rule, throughout this century.

The shell keep, however, was not confined to England. One of the most important castles for the defence of the Norman frontier was Gisors. It has a chemise in the form of a shell keep on top of a 20 metre high motte – in the centre of which is a small tower keep. These two features date originally from the reign of William Rufus and were built circa 1096. Then, in 1123, Henry I built the outer enceinte wall, where flanking towers were used for the first time in France since the Roman period. Most of these were square and open at the gorge. This latter feature made it difficult for an enemy who had captured one to defend it against the garrison inside who might try to retake it. Roman towers were usually open at the gorge, but later thinking inclined towards building them solid all round. This meant that they formed independent strongholds that could resist even if an enemy had managed to get into the bailey.

The shell keep however, was only a temporary measure and soon faded away. The twelfth century is remembered, as far as military architecture is concerned, for the massive rectangular keeps built by Henry I and Henry II, both in France and England. In a book of this sort there is no space for a gazetteer of all those built, but it is as well to examine one or two. Perhaps the best known is Rochester, sited to guard the crossing of the Medway on the London to Canterbury road. The present bailey defences are based on the stone foundations of a wall built by Bishop Gundulf in around 1098. The actual great keep also had episcopal inspiration, as it was constructed by Archbishop William de Corbeil some 30 years later. It can be regarded as typical of the later Norman and early Plantagenet keeps, rising to a height of some 25 metres (82 ft). The ground plan is almost square, but with a projecting small-keep on one side which housed the stairs to the first floor entrance. The porch was originally fronted by a drawbridge, and inside, there was a portcullis across the entrance to the main block. At each corner there is what looks like a tower, but these were simply thin strip buttresses carried up above the height of the roof to form turrets. They had no flanking capability, but were often used to house internal staircases in keeps of this type. The apertures in the upper floors were windows, but in a Norman keep any loophole-like openings in the lower storeys were for ventilation only – the idea of low-level archery was to come later.

The visitor to Rochester will notice, however, that one of the corner turrets is round, which is a mute testimony to one of the main weaknesses of that type of building. When the castle was besieged by King John in 1215, the attackers spent two futile months in bombarding the place with siege engines. They then decided to have recourse to the ancient technique of undermining, and hollowed out a cavity under the corner angle of one of the towers. This excavation was shored up by wooden props, and filled with combustibles – which included in this case, forty of the fattest sub-standard pigs. This unusual but effective mixture was then ignited, the props burnt away, and down came the tower – no doubt to the immense satisfaction of the onlookers. When the castle was rebuilt after the siege, the square tower was no longer in fashion, and it was replaced by a round one.

Other rectangular keeps belonging to the earlier part of the twelfth century are those at Carlisle, Norwich and Castle Hedingham. The strength of such buildings lay in their very solidity. The larger ones were divided by a lateral cross wall, and as I have already said, the basement was used for storage. The correct technical name for a keep was the French word donjon. This has been corrupted in English into dungeon, a prison. Any person who owns a castle today and opens it to the public, is obliged to provide a dungeon for the edification of the visitors, who expect one for their money. Most castles would have had a place to lodge prisoners, but not necessarily every underground chamber was a cell. On the first floor was usually the hall, the centre of daily life for the lord and his followers. There, justice would be dispensed, and the great feasts of the church celebrated. Windows, for obvious reasons were small, and in winter, the fireplaces would have given an illusion of smoky warmth. Small chambers let into the thickness of the walls would have given some privacy, and latrines were provided – usually simply emptying into the moat. Living in such a keep would not have been very comfortable, and the prevailing dampness of the stonework must have caused much suffering from such ailments as rheumatism.

Thus the situation in England in the middle of the century as far as castles were concerned was that the motte and bailey castle still dominated the landscape, although modified in some cases with a shell keep and/or a stone bailey wall. Additionally there were a number of keep and bailey castles, most of which were the property of the king. Following the death of Henry I however, there intervened a period of anarchy, the result of the disputed succession. This was described graphically thus by the *Anglo-Saxon Chronicle* – 'For every great man built him castles and held them against the King [Stephen]; and they filled the whole land with these castles. They sorely burdened the unhappy people of the country with forced labour on the castles; and when the castles were built, they filled them with devils and wicked men.' This was of course written by a monk, who was naturally prejudiced, but probably represented fair comment on the part of the have-nots of the period. The writer then goes on to describe gruesome tortures that were inflicted. The castles referred to in the quote were known as 'adulterine', and it was one of the first duties of Henry II to have them destroyed. They would though, have been of the motte and bailey type – quick and cheap to build, and just as easy to destroy afterwards. Such periods of internal disturbance in the Middle Ages, were always characterized by frantic castle bulding, which only the advent of a strong king could terminate.

Henry II was a great king as far as England was concerned, in respect of his administrative and legal reforms. He was also a great builder of castles. He continued the tradition of building massive rectangular keeps, the most notable being that at Dover which still stands in all its solitary majesty on the White Cliffs above the harbour. As a portent of the future however, at the same time he surrounded his keep with an inner bailey wall that had rectangular flanking towers, a sign that defensive emphasis was moving away from reliance on a passive refuge. Other examples of his keeps were at Bamborough, Newcastle, the Peak and Scarborough – a sign that Royal power was being surely extended into the north. As well as this traditional architecture however, his reign was characterized by a certain amount of experiment. Between 1165 and 1173, he built the keep at Orford in Suffolk, on a totally new site where there had been no previous castle – the reason being the need to curb the ambitions of the Bigod family in the area. The result was an odd shape, cylindrical inside and polygonal on the outside, supported by three massive buttresses. It is obvious that this was not regarded as the answer for the future, for after it was finished, rectangular keeps were still being started – Dover and Helmsley in 1180. The military mind has been traditionally resistant to change, and it is possible that such experiments were regarded with derision.

But why build round shapes rather than square ones? I have already given the reasons, but summarize them again. The angles of a square shape were particularly vulnerable to mining and to the impact of projectiles – for example Rochester. In addition, the interior of a round tower was easier to vault in stone, which reduced the fire hazard from wooden floors. Finally, less masonry was required for a given area, and the shape caused projectiles to be deflected.

Far more interesting than Orford, was Conisbrough in Yorkshire built between 1180 and 1190 by a half-brother of Henry II. The dominant feature was a cylindrical keep built up from an outward splayed plinth. This had the advantage of providing the base of the tower with a much thicker girdle of masonry to deter the miner. The tower itself however, was supported by five massive buttresses symmetrically arranged around the circumference – it has been said that the designer set out to construct a pure cylindrical keep and then lost his nerve. The advantages of the round shape were negated by the buttresses which would have provided even more dead ground and severely hindered the fire of the defenders on the roof. What is even more remarkable about the castle at Conisbrough, however, is the curtain around the bailey, which was flanked by semicircular projecting towers, likewise with splayed plinths. This was an enormous advance on the enceinte at Ludlow as well as the contemporary work at Dover.

This design for the curtain at Conisbrough shows that the much older Roman ideas had definitely reappeared in England, but not until almost a hundred years after the first Crusade, and in spite of existing examples at Pevensey and Portchester. From this one can only assume that until the end of the twelfth century, no real need was felt for a strong curtain. The probable reason for the interest shown in the 1180s was that it was becoming apparent that the increase in power of siege engines meant that they had to be kept further away from the keep. If the bailey could be easily battered down and overrun, the garrison could only hole up in the keep where their capitulation was only a matter of time. The advantage in war was beginning to swing tentatively in favour of the attacker. The man who decided to build an elaborate curtain around his castle, however, had to bear in mind that the greater the perimeter to be defended, the larger the garrison that was required.

Thus we have the traditional rectangular form being built while experiments with other forms were in progress. It was not until 1200, when William Marshall built the great cylindrical keep at Pembroke, that the new shape became permanently established. In point of fact, most of the new keeps were built along the Welsh border, an area of almost perpetual warfare, and where those responsible were more likely to be receptive to innovations.

Having dealt at some length with developments in England, we must now look to the continent, and especially to France. In the eleventh century there had apparently been little stone building carried out in the Duchy of Normandy, but after a raid by the French king into the disputed border territory of the Vexin, Henry I was forced to take steps to improve the defences generally. According to a contemporary account, he built eleven castles in all, among which were Gisors, already mentioned, Domfront, Vire, Arques and Falaise. The original castle at Falaise was where Robert le Diable, Duke of Normandy supposedly wooed Arlette the tanner's daughter, the result of which liaison was William the Bastard, destined to become the conqueror of England. The present castle is a typical Norman rectangular keep with flat buttresses, and the masonry work is of a far higher standard than at Loches for instance.

Experimentation with round forms started much earlier in France than in England, although the rectangular keep lingered on, appearing again at Chambois towards the end of the century – contemporary with Dover. This desire for innovation can perhaps be accounted for in that the Crusades had far more impact in France than elsewhere. At Senlis there was a Gallo-Roman enceinte with circular flanking towers, and the cylindrical keep appeared as early as the mid eleventh century at Fretéval.

The chronicler Jean de Marmoutier tells us that Geoffrey Plantagenet was reading the Roman writer Vegetius at the siege of Montreuil-Bellay in 1151 – a theorist who laid great stress on the value of flanking fire and horizontal defence. As early as 1130, tentative steps in this direction had been taken at Houdan, where a circular keep had been built flanked by four turrets. The designer however, had failed to realise that the curved surfaces between the turrets prevented an accurate cross-fire, besides which he failed to provide any loop-holes at the base of his towers for fire along the curtains. The Tour de César at Provins, built a few years later, suffered from the same defects, as it was octagonal with round towers.

Also of the mid twelfth century, the royal keep at Etampes represents a further step. It was basically a quatrefoil of four towers bonded together to form an extremely strong mass. The same idea was used for Clifford's Tower built on the old motte at York, 50 years later. A further example of these transitional shapes is at Amblény, where the basic four corner towers are joined by extremely short curtains to leave a hollow court in the centre – this was perhaps the prototype of the later extremely popular square fort.

Henry II was also active in his vast dominions in France. He undertook a major rebuild at Gisors, a castle of great strategic importance. Two storeys were added to the central keep, which, with its shell keep chemise, was strengthened with buttresses. The 1123 outer enceinte was improved by the addition of the prominent Devil's Tower. It was his donjon at Niort however, that represented the major innovation in more ways than one – although its design was destined to remain unique. Basically it was two almost identical tower keeps joined by curtains to form a small enclosed courtyard in between. The only entrance to the complex was through a gateway in one of the curtains, and an enemy who penetrated would find himself in an extremely confined space where he would be subject to all the unpleasantness that could be thrown down from above. The keeps themselves were square in ground plan with rounded corner flanking towers, and originally stood in the middle of a vast bailey, the wall of which was flanked by no less than sixteen towers. The most interesting feature of Niort however, was the presence of machicolation on two faces of the southern tower. This brings us to the point where a further basic element of future design first made its appearance in the West.

For a man to lean over the parapet to drop something on those work-ing against the base of the wall was a hazardous undertaking. The first solution to this problem was the provision of hoardings, made of wood, and in the form of galleries that hung out over the battlements. Holes in the flooring could be used for dropping missiles and liquids. In some cases the hoards were roofed over and continued back over the allure – in that case being known as *coursières*. These structures were normally mounted only in times of war, although in some cases there are indications that they were permanent. Several of the German walled cities have their *coursières* in place, and the tower at Laval has an obviously permanent hoarding. There were two methods of mounting. Either holes were left in the masonry just below the parapet into which the joists could be inserted, or they were supported on corbels. The snag was of course, the extreme vulnerability to fire, in spite of various precautions that could be taken. It is thought that the idea first appeared in France in the earlier part of the twelfth century. All that machicolation was, was the replacement of hoardings by similar but permanent constructions in stone. It was probably first used in the Holy Land at Saone, again in the early half of the twelfth century, and its adoption there may have been occasioned by the lack of suitable building timber in that country.

Turning now to the other countries in Europe, there is a fine example of twelfth century work at Ghent in Belgium. This is the castle of the Counts of Flanders, the Gravensteen. This was originally a tenth century stone castle, the lower levels of which form the foundations of the present keep. The castle which we know today, having been extensively restored in the 1880s, was begun in 1180 by Count Phillip – evidently to humble the proud citizenry. Inside was a tower keep and a separate residential building. The surrounding wall overlooking the wet ditch was embellished at a slightly later date with towers corbelled out over the water with two storeys of firing positions inside. These towers were supported on buttresses and in the lower level of each was a pair of latrines opening directly into the ditch – in time of war they could have been used as machicolation apertures, an idea which conjures up all sorts of ribald thoughts.

In Germany, the advent of the Hohenstaufen dynasty of Emperors in 1138, brought a temporary period of comparative stability and strong government. Undoubtedly the greatest of these emperors was Frederick Barbarossa, who died at the end of our period in 1190. The Norman style never caught on in Germany, where there was a continuous tradition going back to Carolingian times. As I mentioned in the last section, the keep or *Burgfried* of the usual German castle was of a non-residential nature, and thus developed in a different way, being often taller and slimmer than an Anglo-Norman type. Barbarossa set out to build a number of magnificent Royal fortresses, which rivalled anything in France and England for beauty of decoration and style. The German designer, not being fettered to the defensive needs of blank walls, could give his imagination free play in constructing elegant palace type residences. These were characterized by wide windowed arcades and ornate interiors.

The Hohenstaufen fortresses had no regular ground plan, being built according to the geography of the site. Trifels, in the Palatinate, is on a hill-top and has the tower and palace compressed into a central block. The surrounding wall was not particularly massive and was unflanked. This however, was not a real necessity in view of the fact that at such a height, no artillery could be brought up the hill to bombard it. A lowland castle in England or France was a different matter, and needed massive outer curtains. One of the best known of Barbarossa's castles is at Nuernberg, where it still stands high above the old city. Although constantly added to over the centuries, much of it is twelfth century, Conrad III started construction on the site of an older castle in 1138, and the work was finished by his nephew and successor, Barbarossa. The *Burgfried* was the massive cylindrical Sinwell Tower, although the superstructure on top dates from the sixteenth century. The main buildings however are grouped around a courtyard, and comprise a palace hall fronted by a fine staircase and an open arcade. There is also a typical two storey chapel – to separate the lower orders from their betters in the sight of God.

Of the other Hohenstaufen fortresses, the Muenzenberg was built on an oblong plateau and featured two large cylindrical keeps, one at each end. This castle remains as an extensive ruin, as does Vianden in Luxembourg. Eger, in Czechoslovakia had a square *Burgfried,* one corner of which projected through the outer wall. The great work at Hagenau in Alsace has disappeared, but at Gelnhausen in Germany, the ruins still display finely decorated windows and doorways.

It is a paradox that in Scandinavia, an area which provided the racial characteristics of the Normans, the art of castle building lagged behind the rest of Europe. The feudal system never really developed, and any work carried out was of a central governmental nature. Although one would have expected the inspiration to have come from Germany, the motte layout seems to have lingered on in Denmark and Sweden until well into the twelfth century. The need for defence seems to have been most apparent on the Baltic coast of Sweden, where a number of stone works were built to fend off heathen pirates.

At this point we must turn to the Crusader castles, and as the majority of the participants were French, it is obvious that their ideas dominated the earlier works built in Palestine. The basic type that first evolved was a keep on a mountain spur, enclosed by a simple curtain. There were, however, certain local conditions that influenced development. One could write not one, but several books on the subject, and space dictates brevity upon what is a fascinating theme. It is important to note the often isolated position of many of them, which meant that they had to be self-sufficient enough to stand a long siege. In addition, their likely Saracen enemies, when united, could always vastly outnumber any army that the Christians could put into the field. Also, in the course of their long struggle with the Byzantine Empire, the Saracens had become masters of siegecraft. All this emphasized the necessity for massive strength, which could in many cases be dispensed with in the small-scale wars in Europe. In such an inhospitable climate, an adequate water supply was also a necessity. It is said that Margat stocked supplies for a garrison of 1,000 men for 5 years.

Most of the Crusader castles are now ruined, although there are impressive remains of several of them. Many were modified at various times by both their Christian builders and the Moslems who later occupied them. Strategically they were sited along the coast, to secure the sea communications with the West, and astride the east-west passes through the mountain chains. There was another group in the south to cover the approaches from Egypt. There again, this strategic sense would have grown up from experience and not from any form of initial master plan worked out in Jerusalem.

The early Crusader castles were not in any sense innovatory – their builders simply used the forms with which they were familiar at home. Many of these works used the rectangular tower, slightly modified to suit local conditions, being often only two storeys high and vaulted rather than having wooden floors. Many of the sites used had remains of earlier Roman work, and in hilly broken country, it was often best to enhance a natural obstacle. Saone, defending the southern approach to Antioch was built in the early part of the twelfth century, astride a rocky promontory. Across this two deep ditches were excavated – or may already have existed – dividing the castle into two sections. The designer, however, built his rectangular keep in the middle of the wall facing the main approach. This was certainly a departure from previous Western practice, where it had been usual to place the keep as far away as possible from the entrance, as a place of last resort. By siting it in the front, the keep became an active unit of the defence, a form of command post from where the *castellan* could direct resistance. This scheme appeared in the West in the next century in the form of the massive gatehouse keep, popular in England.

Margat is on the coast north of Tripoli. Originally taken by the Crusaders in 1117, it remained in feudal ownership until handed over to the Order of the Hospitallers in 1186. It was this order which was mainly responsible for its final form. Perched on the usual mountain ridge, it forms basically the shape of a triangle with the main buildings concentrated at the apex. Its interest lies in that for most of its area, it is enclosed by double walls, the outer one of which was flanked by round towers. Thus the concentric principle seen in the Byzantine city defences was applied to a castle. The outer gate admitted only to a list between the two walls, and any enemy getting through would find himself in a confined space without cover, and subject to the usual shower of missiles from both sides – we have already seen several examples of this type of 'killing area'. To get to the inner gate, the enemy had to move a considerable distance along the list with his right-hand, unshielded side exposed to the main source of fire. In contrast however, to Saone, the cylindrical donjon was at the farthest point of the castle, thus fulfilling the old passive defence rôle.

Another type of Crusader castle, usually on the flat coastal strip, was an adaption of the old Roman legionary camp – a rectangular area of ground enclosed by walls with corner flanking towers. These may of course have been copied from the classical pattern, but could equally well have developed by a process of logic. It was the quickest and cheapest way of defending a military camp.

The most famous, and in many ways the best preserved of the major Crusader castles is Krak des Chevaliers, part of the defensive system covering the Homs gap between Syria and the coast. The Count of Tripoli sold it to the Hospitallers in 1142, who undertook the main rebuilding at the end of the twelfth and the beginning of the thirteenth centuries. The result was a concentric castle with the keep block in the dominant position – a design echoed in some of the Edwardian castles built later in North Wales, although they were more symmetrical. The enceinte of the original castle became the inner wall of the new one, completely overlooking the outer line of the defences. The inner core was made even more difficult of approach by scarping the rocky base into a sloping plinth or talus. Part of the space between the walls was occupied by a reservoir, a defensive obstacle fulfilling a practical need. The entrance followed a sinuous route through a narrow passage and up a ramp with a hairpin bend in the middle. This was defended the whole way by portcullises, doors and *meurtrières* or murder holes in the roof through which missiles could be dropped or liquid poured. As befitted one of the main castles of a military order, it was part fortress, part monastery, and the interior apartments were generous in size and magnificently decorated. The castles of the military orders had a far larger permanent garrison than would have been usual in a western feudal castle, which accounts in part for their large size.

The Crusaders however, were not the only builders of fortifications in the East. The Moslems had also learnt their lessons from the Romans, and constructed large citadels at Aleppo and Damascus, for instance – it was the Crusader failure to take these two cities when they had the opportunity at the time of the First Crusade, that enabled their enemies later to combine to defeat them.

We have already mentioned the appearance of machicolation as a design feature in the Holy Land. Another idea that probably stemmed from there was to build a gallery under the allure fitted with *archères*. This gave an extra level of well protected firing positions. In fact, it is in such smaller details that the Crusades probably exerted their greatest influence on castle building. The twelfth century was the period of pilgrimage to the holy places, combined with the pleasure of smiting the infidel. The Crusader who took the cross was promised all sorts of indulgences for his sins, and the movement proved a useful outlet for the warring energies of the upper classes. As far as the participants were concerned, however, as much as for the heavenly reward, there were also the opportunities for debauchery and loot to provide a martial stimulus.

To conclude our survey of the twelfth century, we must look at Château Gaillard in some detail. This was Richard I's 'saucy' castle, started as a gesture of defiance to the King of France in 1196. Gisors, the cornerstone of the defence of Normandy had been ceded to France by a treaty the year before, leaving the Seine valley open to raids. Richard decided to build on a site overlooking the town of Les Andelys, to cover the approach to Rouen. Several authorities have maintained that Gaillard in its design, heralded a totally new approach, and also have

*Fig. 4   Château Gaillard. Richard Cœur de Lion's gesture of defiance to ·
the King of France.*

described it as being concentric. It should however, be regarded as a culmination of what had been done before, as there was nothing really new about it. It was simply revolutionary in that so many useful features were combined to produce a harmonious entity. Exactly how much of the design can be attributed to Richard is unknown. He was however, one of Europe's foremost warriors and had spent a considerable amount of time both in the East, and in Germany as a prisoner. He did regard Gaillard as his favourite castle, and spent quite some time supervising its construction.

The site was on a spur, only approachable from one direction, and some 200 metres (656 ft) long by 70 metres (230 ft) wide. Thus the defensive emphasis faced all one way and presented a successive series of obstacles to an attacker, whereas a concentric castle was geared to all-round defence. This principle had already been used at La Roche Guyon, further up the Seine. The first obstacle was a triangular outwork or outer bailey, flanked by prominent towers and separated from the main work by a deep ditch. The shape was similar to the ravelin used in seventeenth and eighteenth century artillery fortification, and such a work had been employed by Henry II at Chinon – the Fort St. George. Once through the outer bailey and over the ditch, the attacker was confronted by a massive well-flanked wall that guarded the middle bailey. This in turn gave on to the next obstacle, which was a chemise of unusual construction, around the inner bailey. It was unusual in that it was composed of rounded segments of a circle to produce a scallop-shell effect, supposedly extremely resistant to mining. Inside this, but on the edge of the cliff was a tall round donjon mounted on a forward facing prow or spur. This feature, beside making the lot of the miner more difficult, would have had the effect of deflecting projectiles dropped from above – a form of mediaeval cricket slip-catch. This had also been used at La Roche Guyon. The top of the donjon was machicolated, with the projecting part supported by prominent arches. This in itself produced the desired effect, but would have severely hampered flanking fire. The later form was to mount the gallery on much smaller corbels, although the arched form lingered on for quite some time – it was used as late as the fourteenth century in the Papal Palace at Avignon.

The life of Gaillard was short but eventful as an English possession, and its capture by the French King led directly to the final loss of Normandy. As its siege is well chronicled, it will be discussed in some detail in a later chapter. The castle represents the best example of twelfth century architecture as applied to a work of defence, embodying all that had either been discovered or rediscovered up to that date. Its ruins still stand above the bend of the river at Les Andelys, and it is still possible to gain an impression of what it was like. Warfare however, was progressing all the time, and Richard's pride and joy was obsolete almost as soon as it was finished, a fate that has overtaken so much military equipment.

5

THE GOLDEN AGE OF
THE THIRTEENTH CENTURY

In the last chapter we have seen that a certain number of influences were making themselves felt in castle design, including some from the East. The Roman concept of the rounded tower had been reintroduced, and in countries where warfare was well-organised and a feudal system prevailed, the castle itself was becoming more solid. We have seen that designers were turning their attention to the enceinte, in view of the threat from siege machinery. This new strength given to the outer curtain was to lead in the end to the eclipse of the keep as a necessary feature. As the latter had been the centre of the residential part of the castle, its removal enabled owners to build far more spacious and comfortable apartments sheltered behind their new walls. A new emphasis was also to be placed on active defence, with the strongest parts of the castle being concentrated at the most vulnerable part – the gateway. One can truly say that this was the golden age of castle building, with such great patrons as Phillip Augustus of France, Frederick II, the Hohenstaufen Emperor of Germany, and Edward I of England, all of whom left their imprint on the military architecture of Europe.

After the fall of Château Gaillard in 1204 , Phillip of France managed to mop up the rest of Normandy fairly quickly, with many of the castles surrendering to the king who was obviously going to be the future power in the area. The king of England, John, was incapable of useful intervention, and English barons who had no lands in Normandy saw no reason to fight for the king, in what to them was becoming a foreign land. Phillip however, had to reckon with the fact that not all the local nobility would be in agreement with his takeover, and thus embarked on a crash programme of rebuilding the royal castles, and constructing certain new ones. He added towers to the enceinte at Gisors and Chinon, and built the Talbot Tower at Falaise. This was a tall circular construction some 12 metres (39 ft) in diameter, sited right next to the old rectangular keep, although the frieze on top is fourteenth century machicolation. An interesting feature of these works is that the *archères* are staggered to avoid loss of strength by having them one above the other. Besides the Louvre in Paris, the most important new construction was the castle at Rouen. All that remains of this though, is the Joan of Arc Tower, restored by Viollet le Duc in the nineteenth century. Less well known but far more interesting are the castles at Yèvre le Châtel and Dourdan.

The latter foreshadows the development of the rectangular donjon in France, into what was practically an inner bailey – a shape that was to predominate for the rest of the Middle Ages. In other words, it was a hollow rectangle surrounded by massive walls, against which on the inside, the domestic buildings were grouped. At each corner was a round tower, and in the case of Dourdan, one of these was larger and stronger, becoming in reality an integral keep. The door however, was at ground level, a sure sign of a more active defensive concept. Yèvre le Châtel had a ground plan reminiscent of a squashed diamond, and comprised strong walls linking round towers at the corners. The domestic range was built against one side and occupied nearly half of the area of the bailey. There was no particular keep tower and all four were mounted on solid plinths. The interesting feature is that the wall walk was supported by wide relieving arches, probably copied from Byzantine models. This meant that even if the wall were undermined, it would be unlikely to collapse. Additionally, the wall-walk was continuous with passages cut through the towers at curtain level. This added greatly to the mobility of the garrison during a siege, but could have disadvantages. We have already mentioned the pros and cons of open backed versus closed towers. The usual idea was to use the towers as individual strongpoints isolating each section of curtain with only a narrow staircase to ground level inside. This meant that an enemy on one section of the wall-walk had to fight his way down into the bailey via one tower, and move on to the next one to get on to the next sector of the curtain.

The Yèvre le Châtel school of thought, however, said that mobility for the garrison was more important, and this theme was refined in the design of the slightly later castle at Najac (1250–60). This was one of the most powerful works in the South of France, and stood on the summit of a prominent hill – with a round tower keep forming part of the inner bailey defences. In this respect it was similar to Dourdan, and all the fighting operations of the castle could be controlled from it. As an additional refinement, even if an enemy were in the bailey, the keep could still be closed off by its own ditch and drawbridge at ground level. The wall-walk was continuous, but the passages through the towers could be blocked by removable barriers. All these Phillip Augustus period works however, continued to use hoards rather than machicolations.

During the second quarter of the century, a number of extremely important castles were built in France, the foremost being at Coucy – now a small village to the south of Laon. In the Middle Ages this was a considerable walled township with impressive gateways, and its castle was probably the greatest stronghold ever built by a private person. Its owner's motto was: 'I am neither king nor prince, I am the Lord of Coucy.' The lord in question was Enguerrand III, who built his castle during the minority of Louis XI, and royal minorities at the time were usually a period of hectic castle building by the nobility. The most remarkable feature was the donjon – 'at once the largest, strongest and most magnificent of all mediaeval round towers.' It rose to the impressive height of 60 metres (197 ft) on a diameter of 40 metres (31 ft), and stood outside the main enceinte from which it was separated by its own ditch. This tower was completed in 1240, and although habitable, it is clear that it was regarded solely as a defensive feature for times of need. The main buildings were grouped around the courtyard enclosed within the massive walls which were flanked by drum towers. These included a large hall built on top of open arcades, reminiscent of the Hohenstaufen palaces, and a free-standing church. All had generous windows. 'Neither in France nor elsewhere in the West is there a feudal castle that could compare with Coucy.' Unfortunately for posterity, the castle became a victim of total war in a way which its builder Enguerrand would hardly have understood. In 1917 it was largely destroyed by German artillery, to prevent it being used by the Allies as an observation post.

Contemporary with Coucy, but totally different in conception, was the spectacular stronghold built at Angers, by Blanche of Castile, Regent for the infant King. There is no keep whatsoever, just a massive curtain wall with a perimeter of some 1,000 metres, flanked by no less than seventeen drum towers. The whole work was sited on a solid lump of rock which was scarped to blend in with the outline of the base of the walls and towers. It was thus almost impossible to undermine, but as an added deterrent, the inner bailey was at a higher level than that of the surrounding country outside.

The last of the French works to be discussed at this stage, is Aigues Mortes, although not strictly a castle in the pure sense of the world. It was

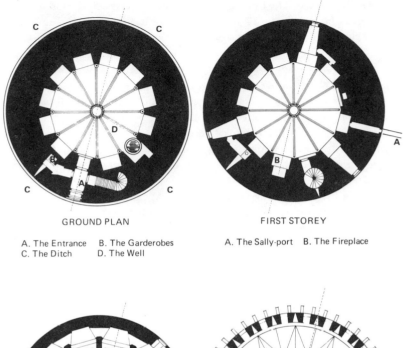

GROUND PLAN

A. The Entrance   B. The Garderobes
C. The Ditch   D. The Well

FIRST STOREY

A. The Sally-port   B. The Fireplace

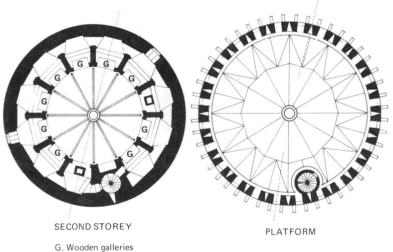

SECOND STOREY

G. Wooden galleries

PLATFORM

Fig. 5   Plans of the keep of Coucy Castle.

originally laid out in the Rhône delta to act as a military base camp for Louis IX's crusade. The first part to be built was the Tour de Constance, between 1241 and 1250. This was a large round tower containing only two interior rooms, and was purely and simply a secure residence for the king. The embrasures on the roof are sixteenth century additions for artillery. Louis himself was never able to complete his plan of enclosing the new camp with walls, and this was left to his son Phillipe le Bel. The resulting work was an almost perfect rectangle with walls flanked by towers – it could in fact have been designed by a Roman engineer, so reminiscent is it of a legionary fortress. This theme continued to be used in the South of France and during warfare with England in Gascony, when a number of military townships were built on the grid pattern – known as *bastides*.

Thus in France, military architecture was taking various forms. The old idea of the totally passive keep was dead, however. Angers was unique and was never emulated on such a scale. Coucy too, with its isolated donjon, had few imitators. The type that was emerging was a rectangular wall enclosing a courtyard within which the domestic buildings were grouped. At each corner would be a tower, one of which might be more prominent and serve as a keep. This however, would be integrated into the defence of the castle and not merely serve as a bolt-hole. It had another purpose though. It could act as a refuge for the owner against an unruly garrison. I shall have more to say about this aspect of the increasing use of mercenaries in castles later on.

During the early part of the century, another great military builder was at large in southern Italy – Frederick II of Germany, warrior, crusader and Holy Roman Emperor, King of Sicily and King of Jerusalem. He returned to the south from his German territories in 1220, and immediately set about reducing numerous private castles. He achieved an adequate administration, from which stemmed a remarkable series of royal works, rivalled only by those built much later by Edward I of England. The castle usually quoted as an example of Frederick's art is the Castel del Monte in Apulia – which was actually more an example of interesting architecture than of a grim and practical fortress. It was conceived as a hunting lodge rather than for any deep strategic purpose, and built circa 1240. In plan it is a regular octagon flanked by eight octagonal towers, the same height as the top of the walls. Probably it was intended to be a keep within a curtain, although the latter was never built. The rooms were arranged

Fig. 6 _Lucera Castle in southern Italy._

against the walls and around a central courtyard – reminiscent of a Norman shell-keep. Frederick's master-builder was a certain Lentini, although most authorities agree that the King himself had a hand in the design of many of his castles. His court reflected both Moslem and Byzantine influences in its life-style – which also is apparent in his architecture. It is classical influence however, that is obvious in the gateway at Castel del Monte, which is flanked by Corinthian columns capped by a pediment. Above this, by way of contrast is a purely Gothic window.

His other works were of a more military character. In southern Italy he was responsible for the castles at Bari, Trani, Termoli and Lucera. The latter, started in 1235, consisted originally of a large tower, mounted on a pyramidal base. Unlike the Norman keep however, there was a courtyard inside, around which were grouped the rooms of the royal residence. The massive surrounding walls of the fortress were added later by Charles of Anjou from 1269 to 1275 – under the direction of a French master-builder. Termoli was a pure tower fortress, again on a pyramidal base, but solid inside. The base itself contained water tanks and storage casemates. In troubled Sicily, Frederick built the castles at Catania and Syracuse, both of which were square and flanked by round towers at the corners – similar to the designs appearing in France at the same time. The difference was one of scale. Catania, which had additional polygonal towers in the middle of each curtain was the work of Lentini, and begun in 1239. Although outwardly powerful, the interior was planned for comfort, with generous rooms featuring the Gothic vault imported from France. At Syracuse there was no courtyard – the centre space was one vast hall divided by twenty-five vaulted arches carried on massive pillars. It has been likened to the hall of a mosque.

We have seen that in England there was a period of experimentation at the end of the twelfth century, ending with hesitant acceptance of the round form – both for flanking and for the keep itself. In 1200, William Marshall added a round tower keep to his castle at Pembroke, which featured a domed roof. This was the tallest and most prominent of the type built in England, due soon to be superseded by other ideas. We have seen that at Conisbrough, the enceinte was flanked by round towers. Another of the early English flanked enceintes was at Framlingham in Norfolk. This was roughly contemporary with Conisbrough, and was built by Hugh Bigod, head of an often turbulent family. An earlier timber castle had been slighted by order of Henry II, who had found it necessary to construct Orford to check the ambitions of the family. During Richard's reign however, Hugh and his successor cheekily rebuilt in stone – a poor man's edition of a Byzantine wall in an irregular circle surrounding a bailey. The site is on top of a mound surrounded by a ditch, and the lengths of straight curtain are flanked by thirteen rectangular towers. These are open at the back and had passages through them at allure level. There was no keep, and the domestic buildings were simply grouped in the bailey. Framlingham is interesting as an early example of a flanked enceinte in this country, but in reality it was obsolete when one considers that the advantages of the round tower had already become apparent.

Apart from turning their attention to the curtain, English castle builders of the early thirteenth century were grappling with the gateway problem – always the weakest part of a castle. A simple tower with a gate and a drawbridge was no longer sufficient, and thought was given to strengthening entrances generally. The logical solution was to multiply the number of barriers that had to be broken down in turn. Portcullises and doors proliferated, as well as *meurtrières* in the roofs of entrance passages. These 'murder holes' had a twofold purpose. Offensively they could be used to drop or pour 'things' on to attackers below – who would try to counter this by lighting a fire to smoke out the defenders in the portcullis winch chamber above. They in their turn had to be well supplied with water to pour down to extinguish the flames. Incidently, the outer portcullis might be left up on purpose. A group of attackers, having battered down the door would then swarm into the passage, to be brought up short by the doors at the other end. The garrison would then drop the portcullis, trapping the enemy inside where they could slaughter them at their leisure.

To strengthen existing gate towers or to enhance new ones, the barbican was increasingly resorted to in this century. This was basically an extension in front of the gate to form an enclosed restricted area. In its simplest form it consisted of two parallel walls built out from the inner entrance and ending in another gatehouse – the effect being to channel attackers into the favoured narrow space. At Lewes, the old Norman gateway was modified in this manner in the late thirteenth century. The new outer gate had a machicolated parapet and corner towers corbelled out from the main block. A similar fourteenth century example is at

Portchester. Another type of barbican was a semi-circular outwork. This was more popular on the continent, and can be seen at both Coucy and Carcassonne. In this country, the West Gate of the Tenby town defences has a semi-circular barbican. Either with or without barbican, the gate had to be flanked, a direct throw-back to Roman practice with D-shaped towers on either side. The entrance at Rockingham, although simple, is a classic example of this design – massively squat towers on either side of a neat arched portal. All these varying solutions of the gateway problem were indicative of the already mentioned desire for a more active defence. The final answer came later in the century, when the gatehouse replaced the keep in the grandeur of its design and the power of its defences.

At this stage we come to the beginnings of the concentric castle in the West. We have seen that the early Crusaders saw examples of the triple wall at Constantinople and the double wall at Nicaea, and used the principle in some of their works in the Holy Land. Its practical development was, like so many features of castle design, in many ways logical. If one had a well-built castle and wanted to make it stronger, the obvious thing to do was to build another ring of walls around it. In theory, the perfect defensive work is symmetrical, so as to be equally strong at all points. In practice however, this was seldom possible to achieve, unless the builder could start from scratch on a perfectly level site. Anybody who has travelled in south-eastern France is sure to have visited Carcassonne, another of Viollet-le-Duc's masterly restorations. The site of the town was originally fortified both in Roman and Visigothic times and had been remodelled in the twelfth century. In 1240, extensive moderations were started, to continue for some 40 years altogether. The

---

Fig 7   *Plan of the Castle of Carcassonne.*

A. The outer gate of the barbican towards the city.

B. Outer gate of castle.

C. The bridge across the moat.

D. The outer barbican.

E. Passage from the outer barbican to the castle.

F. Parapet to protect the gate.

G. Second gate.

H. Third gate.

I. Postern.

J. Passage.

K. Principal courtyard.

L. Small courtyard.

M. Porticoes.

N. Principal gate.

O. Barracks.

P. The keep towers.

Q. Watch-tower.

S. Guard-house.

T. The north gate.

U. Towers.

V. Tower wall.

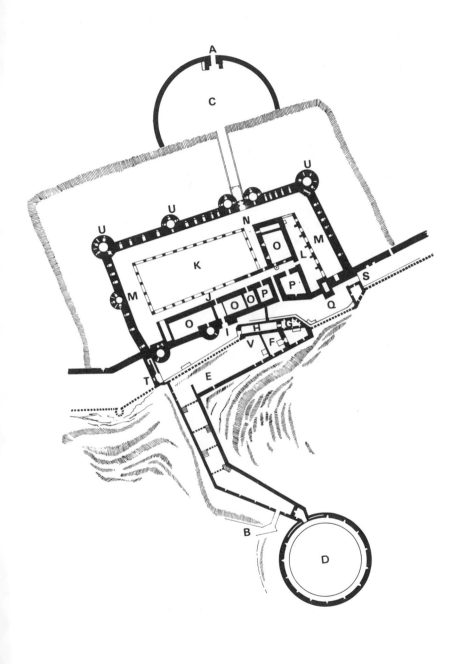

existing curtain was strengthened and some new towers were added. The important addition however, was a new enceinte, leaving a relatively narrow list between it and the original walls, which were higher. The citadel was also improved, with the addition of a barbican extending downhill in front of the walls and closed by a circular outwork. When finished, Carcassonne was the complete mediaeval walled town with citadel, employing every trick of military architecture then known. Its towers however, were rather slim, and have a less powerful effect optically, than the squat form employed elsewhere.

The largest and also one of the earliest concentric castles in Europe is the well-known Tower of London. Originally built by William the Conqueror to overawe the citizens of London, its basis was the White Tower, the first rectangular keep in this country. Under his successors it was developed both as a fortress and royal residence, the keep being surrounded by walls and towers. During the reign of Henry III, an outer enceinte was added exactly parallel to the older inner one, separated from it by a ditch. In fact, so powerful did the rings of walls and towers become, that the White Tower in the middle faded into insignificance as part of the defences. A new emphasis was also placed on the entrance arrangements. A whole series of gates and passages had to be negotiated before the inner bailey could be reached. In course of time, the defences of the Tower became obsolescent, but the structure was retained not only as a notorious state prison, but as the main arsenal of the country as well.

Of the series of great castles in Wales, one was started before the reign of Edward I. A private castle, the property of the Clare family, Caerphilly in South Wales was the most complex non-royal work built in Britain. It was constructed between 1267 and 1277 on an island in the middle of a lake. The stream that fed this was checked by a dam which controlled the level of the water, and at the same time formed the barbican or outwork. The castle itself comprised a low outer bailey rising directly out of the lake. Inside this was the inner bailey surrounded by high walls and boldly projecting towers. Thus the only way to attack the castle other than by mounting an amphibious operation, was to force the barbican and advance across the bridge under fire. Such a large area of water would have been impossible to fill in as a base for siege operations. There was no keep, the main defensive strength being concentrated in the prominent gatehouse. This formed an independent stronghold complete with self-contained accommodation for the *castellan* – it could be held against an enemy from within as well as without. This aspect was becoming steadily more important as the use of feudal troops declined, only to be replaced by mercenaries. Those with feudal obligations for castle guard preferred in many cases to settle with the lord for a money payment in lieu. Hired soldiers, however, had the habit of rioting if left without pay.

'These drew not for their fields the sword,
Like tenants of a feudal lord,
Nor owned the patriarchal claim
Of chieftain in their leader's name;
Adventurers they, who far from roved,
To live by battle which they loved.
In camps licentious, wild, and bold;
In pillage fierce and uncontrolled;
And now, by holytide and feast,
From rules of discipline released.'   Sir Walter Scott.

An interesting feature of Caerphilly is that it has a number of postern gates. This is another of the indications of active defence, giving the chance for the garrison to sally out to take the attackers in the rear and to hamper their siege operations. In a sally, the mounted knight came again into his own.

The earlier castles of Edward I in Wales did not exhibit the sophistication of the later ones, although only 18 years separated Flint from Beaumaris. The former was a throw-back to an earlier period, and could even have been inspired by Coucy. The main feature was a cylindrical keep at one corner of the enceinte, but separated from it by its own ditch, while the other corners were flanked by drum towers. Flint was started in 1277, the same year as Rhuddlan. This was also an unsatisfactory work, although described by one authority as a simple but perfect concentric castle. The inner bailey enceinte had a trapezoid plan with drum towers at the two most salient angles, and flanked gateways at the other two corners. The outer enceinte however, was weak by comparison, irregular in shape, and parts of it were up to 70 metres (230 ft) away from the inner bailey wall. This left plenty of room for an enemy to concentrate out of range of really heavy fire.

The Edwardian castles in Wales have been criticized for having been like sledgehammers built to crack walnuts – the nuts in question being the lightly armed Welsh tribesmen. Edward, however, was an experienced warrior, and would hardly have expended so much money and effort if he had not thought it justified. Unlike so many castles, we know the name of the man who was responsible for the Welsh works, a Savoyard by the name of James St. George. Eight major castles were built in all, several of them in conjunction with new towns set up to establish an English presence in the captured territories. These townships were designed largely on the grid pattern that reappeared at Aigues Mortes and in the *bastides* in France. Except for Aberystwyth and Builth, they were all in the north and accessible by water – an early example of English sea power used for strategic purposes. Even if cut off by the local population they could still have been supplied by the fleet. Right from the start, there appears to have been a general strategic concept in the siting of the works, designed to pen the Welsh into the wastes of Snowdonia. This was a departure from the previous haphazard tactical placing of castles.

The two most imposing works were Conway and Caernarvon, both of which were built on irregular sites and demonstrated their power by the massive strength of the enceinte defences. They also formed citadels in conjunction with fortified towns. Conway stands on a long narrow finger of rock, and thus could not have been built in concentric form anyway. It used the Gaillard principle of opposing a line of successive obstacles to an attacker. Thanks to impeccable accounting, we have a good idea of the progress of the work and its cost to the exchequer. In all, an amount of around £14,000 was spent over a period of 8 years, starting in 1283 – in modern terms, perhaps in the order of £3,000,000. Both north and south faces are flanked by four large drum towers, and the castle is divided into two baileys or wards, the inner and the outer. The former contained the royal apartments, while the latter housed the great hall, kitchen, and stables etc. The main entrance was to the west via a barbican. The visitor had to climb a ramp, cross a drawbridge and then go up a narrow flight of steps into the barbican. From there he had to make an abrupt left turn through the flanked gateway into the outer ward. To approach the inner ward there was a further drawbridge and a dog-leg turn through the dividing wall. A somewhat non-English feature are the turrets on top of the towers around the inner ward. They served no particularly useful military purpose, except in that they enhanced the impressiveness of the silhouette – the main towers were high enough for normal look-out needs. Impressiveness however, was important in a castle built to dominate a conquered people.

Caernarvon, started in the same year, is similar but different. In fact, it is odd that although they shared the same designer, Conway had round towers and Caernarvon had polygonal ones. Mediaeval military architects never managed to introduce any form of standardization into their creations. Caernarvon was intended as the seat of government for the new principality, but although work was in progress for 50 years, it was never fully finished. The shape was akin to an hour-glass, and the towers were astride the line of the walls, whereas at Conway they projected only outwards. This brings us back to the great wall-walk debate. At Conway it was continuous, while at Caernarvon, each tower was a separate strongpoint – also commanding the interior.

The last two Edwardian castles to be considered are Harlech and Beaumaris, both of them concentric, and the latter being the most symmetrically perfect design ever built. Anything that came after Beaumaris was in many ways an anti-climax. Harlech occupies a hill site, and has a lower middle bailey surrounding a much higher inner one. The outer bailey was an irregular shape that straggled down the hill and was of no great strength. There was only one main entrance to the inner bailey, via a truly massive gatehouse that rivals any Norman keep in strength and size. Not only flanked at the front, it had two further flanking towers inside to cope with a mutinous garrison. In addition, the system of doors and portcullises leading in from the front, was duplicated from the rear.

The irony of Beaumaris, the perfect design, was that it was never finished, and St. George, who died in 1309, would have never seen his masterpiece completed anyway. In 1294, Caernarvon in unfinished state at the other end of the Menai Strait was captured by the Welsh and held by them for 6 months. Perhaps as a form of overkill, Beaumaris was started on the Anglesey side of the Strait as soon as order had been re-established. Its genesis from Harlech is obvious, but being on level ground it was possible to build the ideal symmetrical shape. The inner bailey is defended by six towers, and like Caerphilly, has a gatehouse at each end. Each of these was defended by three portcullises, two doors and numerous *meurtrières*. The outer wall was added later, between 1316 and 1320, and unlike Harlech, was itself flanked by a number of small round towers.

An odd feature of all the Edwardian castles is their complete lack of machicolation – it is obvious that St. George thought this neither necessary nor desirable. It is however doubly odd, that when one considers that he strove for a strong visual effect on the skyline, he should have ignored the value of machicolation as a decorative element. He did, however, employ the Crusader idea of loop-holed galleries under the parapet.

Before leaving the British Isles, there are one or two further castles that should be mentioned. Military architecture in Wales, even before Edward I's 'final solution' had always been of great importance, and had often reached a higher state of development than in England. (This was due, of course, to the state of almost perpetual warfare.) Kidwelly Castle, like Caerphilly, was a great baronial stronghold, started around 1275. Semi-circular in shape, it is concentric around the curved side. Like some of the royal works, it was the focal point of a walled town, which formed in effect, an outer bailey. The main entrance was to the south, which was guarded by the inevitable massive flanked gateway. Once inside, the space between the baileys was fairly open, but still restricted enough to prevent an enemy from establishing himself. The inner kernel was enclosed by massive walls flanked by round towers at the corners, while from the straight side of the enceinte, the apse of the chapel projected.

One of the border or Marcher castles was Goodrich, guarding a crossing of the river Wye. Its towers were strengthened by extensive spurs at the base, which can still be seen in spite of the ruinous state of the work as a whole. What is particularly interesting about the castle is that in the middle is a Norman rectangular keep, once the pride of the owner, but dwarfed into insignificance by the sheer size of the thirteenth century enceinte surrounding it.

After the Welsh, it was the turn of the Scots to be invaded from the south. Their castles were less impressive and fell easily to the intruder. A solution similar to that imposed in Wales, however, was impossible, mainly for financial reasons. There was simply no more money left in the treasury to garrison the Lowlands on such a scale as North Wales.

There are nevertheless three impressive thirteenth century Scottish castles. Bothwell was another of the type probably inspired by Coucy, with a round tower keep – but astride the main enceinte rather than separate from it. It did though have its own ditch, and the entrance was from the inner bailey via a drawbridge. Bothwell was built in the 1270s, but in 1239, Alexander II of Scotland had married Marie, daughter of Enguerrand III of Coucy. It is thus possible that the inspiration was direct rather than by hearsay.

Caerlaverock was a rarity in that it had a triangular ground plan and quite definite French influence – with its machicolated tower parapets and proliferation of miniature turrets or bartizans. To continue the French analogy, originally it had steeply pitched conical roofs on the towers. Scotland has always been traditionally bound to France, and in the 'Auld Alliance', it is not difficult to see the reason behind the French flavour of so many Scots castles. The apex of the triangle at Caerlaverock is secured by a massive gatehouse, which at the same time forms the fighting front of the castle. Although slighted during the Civil War period, it is remarkably complete. Begun in 1290, and thus contemporary with the Welsh castles, it was taken by the English in 1300.

It is known that James St. George was in Scotland shortly before his death, and the keep gatehouse at Kildrummy can probably be ascribed to him. It is in fact, remarkably similar to the one at Harlech, although the castle itself as a whole, with its semi-circular ground plan, is more like Kidwelly.

Before leaving the castles of Edward I, mention should be made of the fact that during his reign, certain works were built in the Bordeaux area. The most important of these was the castle of Blanquefort, which stands on level ground in a flat marshy plain. Rectangular, and without a keep, it is flanked by six heavy round towers, which were originally surrounded by hoardings. The interesting feature however, is that the towers did not rise above the level of the walls, so that the entire top of the castle was a single fighting platform – a type that was only to become popular in France quite some time later. The curtains were defended by prominent arched machicolations, similar to the much earlier ones at Niort and Gaillard.

Elsewhere in Europe, the development of military architecture was slower and less spectacular. The main reason for this, as mentioned before, was lack of large enough administrative units with the necessary resources for large scale building. After the eclipse of the Hohenstaufen emperors in Germany, the power of the Empire declined, which accentuated the split into petty principalities. This was very much the era of the robber baron with his castle perched on a crag, exacting tribute from all who passed. This particularly hit the rapidly emerging towns whose prosperity was based on long distance trade. The basic types of German castles remained the same, with the wall adapted to the terrain being the most popular among the lesser nobility – it was cheaper and more easy to maintain, and usually only one front had to be defended. The provision of flanking fire was never carried in the German countries to the same extent as in France and England. The towers were usually slender and high, rather than being of the squat drum shape. Walls generally were also much thinner. The other type, normally on a conical hill that needed to be defended from all sides, retained the central defence scheme with the tower in the middle. Many earlier works were supplemented by another ring of walls lower down the hill, making them in effect into concentric castles. The general impression of German fortresses however, is of buildings thrown together from various periods, without any real defensive concept. In their favour of course, is the fact that their sites were often so inaccessible as to make the need for serious defence minimal.

In Switzerland and Austria, the development broadly speaking was similar. The best known of the Swiss castles is undoubtedly Chillon, on the shore of Lake Geneva, which was popular with romantic poets.

> There are seven pillars of Gothic mould,
> In Chillon's dungeons deep and old;
> There are seven columns massy and gray,
> Dim with a dull imprisoned ray. . . .   Lord Byron

These lines from *Childe Harold* refer to the famous prisoner of Chillon, and the seven pillars can still be seen in the basement of the castle. Chillon was originally the main residence of the Counts of Savoy, and probably started out as a simple tower on an island close to the shore. In the eleventh century, an enceinte was added, as well as the Tower of the Dukes. The main building phase was in the 1260s, and was undertaken for Count Peter II. This worthy gentleman had strong connexions with England, being related by marriage to Henry III and holding the title of Duke of Richmond. It is possible that the Savoyard James St. George came to this country via that connexion. The strategic importance of Chillon lay in the fact that it was on the main route to the St Bernhard Pass. On the land side it became concentric through the addition of a second line of walls flanked by towers, and featured a solid stone plinth running through this outer line and up the intervening terrace to the inner wall. The interior of the bailey was divided into two by the old donjon tower.

The Low Countries have always been a convenient battlefield, and there too, castles proliferated in the thirteenth century – adapted to the peculiarities of the terrain. Many of them feature water defences, and exhibit both German and French influence. The square fort appeared in the Netherlands at this time, and the best restored example is certainly the Muiderslot at Muiden close to the Ijssel Meer. Built like so many in the area, of brick, the original castle was constructed around 1285. It has four round corner towers capped by steeply pitched conical roofs. The entrance is guarded by a high square gatehouse facing the moat, approachable over a bridge. The rear of the inner courtyard is occupied by a hall-residence as high as the surrounding curtain, which also had a steep roof.

The earliest type of castle in the Low Countries, was simply the ring wall. The twelfth century *Burcht* at Leiden is an example, almost akin to an English shell keep. It acted however, purely as a refuge, as there were no residential buildings inside. In the thirteenth and fourteenth centuries, many of these ring wall castles were modified by the addition of flanking towers. Another type that emerged late in the thirteenth century, and was to become somewhat of a pattern for the lesser nobility, was the simple tower house – a residence that could be defended against marauders, but not against an army.

To conclude this survey of thirteenth century military architecture, we must briefly turn to a group of German castles that in many ways were totally ungermanic in origin. These were the works built by the Order of the Teutonic Knights, in Prussia and the Baltic states. Like the Hospitallers, the Order was founded in the Holy Land during the Crusades, in 1198. The drive to the East, to Christianize the Slavs and other peoples in the region started in 1230, although the early castles built were merely impermanent structures. The main building phase lasted from 1260 to 1290, and the external architecture was decidedly North German, as was the brick construction. Like the other two military orders, the Teutonic Knights were immensely wealthy, and the large scale of their works reflected the need for a combination of fortress and monastery. The basic type that developed was based around the convent house, a rectangle of four blocks around a courtyard containing the necessary public rooms – refectory, dormitories, chapel etc. Marienburg in Prussia was the residence of the High Master of the Order, and originally consisted only of the *Hochschloss* which was the convent house. The other parts were added in the next century, reflecting a very real sense of gracious living. A more military structure was Rheden. This had the rectangular convent house in the middle of a square island, the edge of which was defended by a wall, making it concentric. The whole castle was surrounded by a moat, but there was little flanking capacity – perhaps it was not felt to be necessary. The emphasis was more on decoration, but a solid watch tower gave the castle a military appearance. The Bishops' palaces too were influenced by the style of the Order. Marienwerder in West Prussia also reflected this strange mixture of military necessity and ornate comfort. Of enormous height and with steep roofs pierced by dormer windows, its sheer magnificence must have greatly impressed the local heathen. Although these works have to be included in any general summary of European castles, the writer has never been able to regard them as serious military works.

With the end of the thirteenth century, the castle had reached its peak as far as defensive capability was concerned. Many more continued to be built right up to the end of the Middle Ages, but social, military and economic factors were to combine to change the emphasis away from defence. These developments will be charted in some detail in the next chapter.

6

THE DECLINE OF THE CASTLE

The Edwardian castles in Wales represented the high point of mediaeval fortress design in Europe. Anything that came afterwards was but an anti-climax from a military point of view, and it was after all, for military purposes that they were built. Once the residential predominated over the defensive, the result was no longer a castle, but a country house or a palace. The reasons for this change are several, although the usual answer is the advent of firearms. This factor however, did not change the art of warfare overnight, and the earlier cannon were probably more dangerous to their own crews than to the enemy. They would have had though, a certain effect on morale, on account of the noise they generated. All sorts of dates are given for the invention of cannon, mostly around the 1320s, but it can be safely said that they were in the arsenals of the more powerful monarchs by the 1350s. By 1400, the cannon had become a powerful battering agent, but it was not absolutely perfected as a destroyer of castles until the Italian campaign of Charles IX of France in 1494. The earlier guns were used entirely in an anti-personnel rôle, discharging at first arrows, and only later iron balls and stones. In 1377 however, Froissart in his chronicle records the use of cannon by the Duke of Burgundy to batter the town of Odruik. So successful were they, that the English commander surrendered apparently because of the effect that the 200 lb stone projectiles had had on his walls. From this time onward, there are frequent references to successful bombardments. Guns nevertheless were expensive and specialist knowledge was required for their manufacture and use. Thus they were reserved for the rising monarchies, and never became the playthings of the feudal nobility.

The castle pure and simple, with its twin elements of fortress and residence really came to the parting of the ways with the decline of feudalism. We have seen how the limited period of service of a feudal army led to an increasing employment of mercenaries – who cost money and were often unreliable. In addition, the owner of a castle who had earlier garrisoned it with his sworn retainers, also had to have recourse to hired troops – who were not bound to him personally by the old ties of neighbourhood and loyalty. The nation states were expanding, and in their train came often successful campaigns to limit the powers of the old nobility. A new class of wealthy bourgeois was appearing in Europe, rising through royal patronage, and in addition to this, culture and economic life was increasingly being concentrated in the towns. The feudal system had been essentially a form of barter – protection in return for goods and services – and based on agriculture. The rise of a money economy changed all this, with feudal obligations being remitted in return for cash payments.

The very sophistication of military architecture by the end of the thirteenth century meant that great castles could no longer be built except by the enormously wealthy, which meant in practice, the monarchies. Royal control also succeeded in banishing much of the private feuding that had been inherent in mediaeval life. Thus the tendency appeared for the nobility either to convert their existing castles into more spacious and comfortable country houses, or to abandon them and build totally civilian structures. The pure stronghold swung through the full circle and became once again a matter of national concern to be maintained by the government.

These changes however, did not occur overnight, and a vast amount of castle building was still in progress during the period with which we are concerned. The aforementioned factors however must be borne in mind.

In 1300, several of the Edwardian castles in Britain were still unfinished. Other types appeared however, and castles continued to be constructed throughout the country. One of the immediate results of Edward's incursion into Scotland was to create an area of tension along the border, with regular raiding from both sides. Previously the area had not been generally fortified, except for the main castles such as Berwick, Carlisle, Alnwick and Bamborough. The changed circumstances however, created a defensive need on the part of the lesser gentry – who had neither the resources nor the requirement for massive works. The result was the construction of a large number of Pele towers all over the northern counties of England and the Lowlands of Scotland. They were basically residential towers, often with the entrance above ground level, and surrounded by a palisaded enclosure known as a barmkin. Thus in some ways we have a reversion to the old motte and bailey castles –

Fig. 8   Fourteenth century Doonenburg Castle in the Netherlands.

without the motte. This does not mean that the inhabitants of the Borders were consciously imitating the early Normans. A palisaded enclosure was logical, to house cattle etc., and to ward off lightly armed raiders, the tower house was the cheapest and best solution. The basic mediaeval unit for living was the hall house, and in many ways, the tower was the same thing turned up on end. When the need for defence declined, the tower house disappeared, leaving us with the basic shape of our modern residences spread out rather than built upwards.

Pele towers came in all sizes and degrees of splendour. Basically, like a rectangular keep, they consisted of a ground floor for storage, a first floor hall and second floor private apartments. Some of them, like the Vicar's Pele at Corbridge in Northumberland, were simple structures with few pretensions to style. On the other hand, Chipchase, likewise in Northumberland, had a full machicolated frieze and corbelled-out corner turrets. This was all very French, but more decorative than useful.

A castle built entirely at one time is a comparative rarity. Most of them have been added to at so many different times that it is usually difficult for the layman to decide what is original and what is not. Thus it was that many castles at this time lost their forbidding aspect, as in pursuit of comfort, new and more spacious buildings were added inside. Curtain walls were pierced by large windows, and complicated chimney stacks came to dominate the skyline – rather than crenellated turrets. A case in point, and a paradox at that, is Warwick Castle. On the one hand, the town side was strengthened militarily during the latter part of the fourteenth century, while at the same time, the older domestic buildings were entirely replaced on a far more lavish scale. The new fortification at Warwick was probably the last example of truly massive defensive architecture with serious military purpose, to be carried out in this country. Firstly, a fine gatehouse was constructed, rising three storeys above the entrance level, with the usual pair of flanking towers. In front of this, a barbican consisting of parallel walls forming a narrow passage was built out. The whole entrance system was covered by a multiplicity of portcullises, doors and *meurtrières*. The two most striking features indeed, were the towers at either end of the gatehouse curtain. Guy's Tower, 43 metres (141 ft) high, was a polygonal structure with a boldly machicolated parapet. Caesar's Tower, on the other hand, was of a three lobe trefoil shape, and slightly higher at 49 metres (161 ft). It too had a machicolated parapet surmounted by a crenellated turret. Such high towers were a rarity in England, and may have been inspired by French ideas. All these new works at Warwick were carried out by the Beauchamp earls, proving that the nobility still had enough power to be able to build on such a scale. At the same time, however, neighbouring Kenilworth was being transformed entirely into a palace, with but few claims to being a defended place.

Still very much a military building is Bodiam, in Sussex, perhaps one of our most beautiful castles as far as the site is concerned. The licence to crenellate, the royal permission for a private person to fortify his dwelling, was granted in 1385 – for the express purpose of defending the area against French raids. The owner, Sir Edward Dalyngrigge, was a veteran of the French wars – one of those who had made good and returned with enough plunder to set himself up in style. He placed his new castle in the middle of a broad lake, just off the river Rother, at that time navigable. Bodiam is a quadrangular castle with the inevitable strong round towers at the corners. The two longer sides have additional square towers in the middle. The main entrance at the north has a fine gatehouse flanked by towers, and the approach was originally across the lake via an artificial causeway. This ran parallel to the main walls on to an island, where the visitor had to make a sharp right turn to approach the gate through a barbican – still on the causeway, which had the additional hazard of several drawbridges. To the south, there was a less complicated entrance acting as a postern. Inside, the buildings are grouped around an open courtyard – hall, kitchen, chapel and retainers' quarters. It is interesting to note that the latter had no internal communication with the lord's apartments or the gatehouse block. Bodiam is open to the public, and we owe its preservation to Lord Curzon (1859-1925), one time Viceroy of India, who bought it and restored it at his own expense before presenting it to the nation.

While Bodiam was a fairly standard design, probably inspired by its owner's stay in France, another coast defence castle, slightly earlier in date, was unique. Queenborough Castle, on the Isle of Sheppey in Kent, was a royal building, both concentric and circular. Although destroyed, drawings have survived. It was started in 1361, and named after Queen Phillipa, the wife of Edward III. The outer enceinte was a perfectly circular wall surrounded by a ditch. This had a postern and a main entrance flanked by towers. The inner bailey was in some ways reminiscent of a shell keep – a circular wall flanked by six round towers, with the domestic apartments arranged around the central courtyard. The ingenuity lay in the approach arrangements. Once through the main gatehouse, the would-be attacker found himself in a narrow passage which ended in a blank wall against the inner bailey curtain. The only way out was through openings in either side of this passage, leading into the space between the two concentric walls. To get to the entrance of the inner bailey the attacker then had to move 180 degrees around the list, exposed to fire from both sides, and then enter another passage and finally force the gate.

Lawlessness continued to prevail in the north until well into Tudor times. Pele towers were still being built in the sixteenth century in Scotland. Wales however, was more or less subdued by the Edwardian conquest, and serious castle building ceased in the fourteenth century. The exception however, is Raglan Castle which was started in the early part of the fifteenth century – a vast pile of masonry combining residential and military usage. It was stoutly defended for Charles I during the Civil War, which accounts for its present day ruinous appearance. The builder was a certain Sir William ap Thomas, the Blue Knight of Gwent, another of the veterans of the French wars, who in addition had had the good fortune to marry money. The fact that Thomas was a parvenu must be the sole justification for the building of what, in strictly military terms, was akin to a folly. There could have been no justification in terms of security from the odd marauders for such an example of defensive 'overkill'. The site had probably been originally occupied by a motte and bailey castle, and the two resulting courtyards would have been the original bailey. These courts were surrounded by high curtains dominated by prominent machicolated towers. The glory, or if you prefer it, the crowning anachronism, was however, the Yellow Tower of Gwent. This was separate from the main enceinte and sited within its own ditch. The five storeyed hexagonal tower was originally over 30 metres (98.4 ft) high and crowned by a machicolated frieze. The base diameter was 20 metres (65.6 ft) and was surrounded by a crenellated berm or *fausse braye* which had six small turrets. This idea of a separate keep was in the style of Coucy, Flint and Bothwell, and its only possible justification in the fifteenth century could have been the need for a refuge from an unruly garrison.

In southern England, the tower house also made a reappearance, although for different reasons to those built in the north. Architecturally by far the most satisfying is Nunney, not far from Frome in Somerset. This again was constructed by one of the lesser nobility who had fought during part of the Hundred Years War, and also seems to have fulfilled a coast defence rôle. The licence to crenellate was issued in 1373, but like so many fine castles, it was slighted during the Civil War. Its inspiration was certainly French as far as the exterior embellishments were concerned, and because of the lack of large outside windows, it is clear that it was expected to fulfil a military purpose. Basically, Nunney was a four storey rectangular keep, with wooden floors and generous rooms. At each corner however, was a stout drum tower with bold corbelled machicolation. Originally the towers would have had the typically French conical roofs, while the centre of the block had a gabled roof with dormer windows. The whole block is built on a narrow berm in the middle of a wet ditch. Some moated castles have their walls rising directly from the water, while others are surrounded by a ledge or berm. The purpose of this was to catch any masonry brought down by battering engines, to stop it falling in the moat – where it could be used as a rubble basis for a crossing by the enemy.

Warkworth was one of the strongholds of the Percy family in Northumberland, but was more than a pele tower. Originally it had been a motte and bailey castle, but had been rebuilt over the years in stone with the result that as at Goodrich, the curtain had come to overshadow the keep on the motte. As a frontier castle, the defensive element was still important, and around 1390, the old keep was replaced by a new tower house. In plan it was square, with the addition of a square flanking tower in the middle of each face. This resulted in a cruciform shape similar to that of the much older Norman castle of Trim in Ireland. The centre at Warkworth however, was a hollow lantern, providing an illumination shaft for the generous apartments, and the whole block was surmounted by a tall observation turret. On one of the flanking towers was the proud Percy lion rampant in relief.

Probably the best known of these later tower houses is Tattersall in Lincolnshire, built of brick, the common north European building material. Although it has been claimed that the design was a conscious harking back to the Norman keep, it is more probable that the design originated from Germany or the Low Countries. Through the wool trade, Lincolnshire had strong connexions with that area. The owner, the first Lord Cromwell, was one of the 'new men', a royal official who would seem to have done well out of the perquisites of office. He reconstructed his earlier castle between 1434 and 1446, firstly by providing a range of domestic buildings within the simply defended bailey. On one side of this he had his famous tower constructed, which is still more or less intact – a fantastic architectural achievement for the late Middle Ages. Here also we owe a debt of gratitude to Lord Curzon who restored it for the nation, describing it as 'the most magnificent piece of brickwork in England.' The tower itself rises through four storeys with an octagonal tower at each corner. The parapet is crenellated and machicolated, although defence cannot have been the main thought behind the design, for the west side is pierced by a series of graceful perpendicular windows. Like the Blue Knight of Gwent, Cromwell was a parvenu, and that sort of person seemed to want to ape the trappings of their feudal betters, by demonstrating their wealth in an over ornate manner. When Curzon bought the place, the fine fireplaces had already been ripped out to be sold to America. He combed the antique dealers until he found them, bought them back at an inflated price, and had them restored *in situ*.

The last of the tower houses to be considered is Ashby de la Zouch in Leicestershire. Although often described as a fortified manor house, it is clear from the size and scale of the building that it was something more. Readers may have come cross the term 'bastard feudalism'. This refers to the private armies of retainers kept in castles in return for livery and maintainance. Unemployed soldiers from mercenary companies were often happy to take service with a powerful lord, and such armies thrived during the period of the Wars of the Roses. With the return of powerful government under the first Tudor, Henry VII, stern measures were taken against this menace to authority, with the result that it was stamped out. Ashby was a product of bastard feudalism, started as late as 1474. The owner was Lord Hastings, who reconstructed an earlier manor, and added on the tower to one side. Originally some 30 metres (98.4 ft) high, its present ruined state is due to a siege during the Civil War. The castle also featured prominently in Sir Walter Scott's *Ivanhoe*. Internally, the apartments had a high standard of finish, and the tower could be completely isolated from the rest of the buildings.

Before moving on to the continent, we must turn to Herstmonceaux in Sussex, not far from Bodiam and built on a similar plan. In the design there is no trace of the tower idea, but rather a return to the

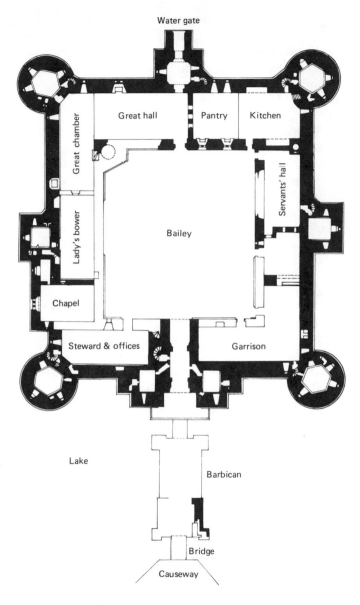

Water gate

Great hall

Pantry

Kitchen

Great chamber

Servants' hall

Lady's bower

Bailey

Chapel

Steward & offices

Garrison

Lake

Barbican

Bridge

Causeway

Fig. 9 Ground floor plan of Bodiam Castle, Sussex.

quadrangular castle. It is an exact contemporary of Tattersall and likewise built of brick. It is also similar in that it represents a display of feudal pride complete with all the trappings of military architecture. Tradition demanded that the wealthy should house themselves in castle-like structures where the semblance of defence was preserved, but the skin was far too thin to have been able to withstand a serious siege. Herstmonceaux has bold octagonal corner towers and a magnificent gateway complete with turrets and machicolation. It still sits amid the water lilies in the moat, externally beautifully restored. The interior is part of the Royal Observatory and cannot be visited, which does not really matter as it was gutted in the eighteenth century. The present inside buildings are early twentieth century additions.

Generally, it was the same story on the continent as in England. Design tended to stagnate after 1300, and no new developments were incorporated until the Italians discovered modern artillery defences around 1500. The same social and economic tendencies also applied – the decline of the feudal system coupled with the rise of central authority, and a gradual awareness of the power of artillery. The former, as in England, led in turn to an increased desire for comfort on the part of castle dwellers. We come also to the period of the Renaissance with a new emphasis on learning and art, a period that produced many of the finest châteaux on the Loire and elsewhere in France.

There are however, several examples of late mediaeval castles in France that should be mentioned. Among these are the early fourteenth century Papal works. The first of the Avignon Popes, Clement V (1305–14) was a native of the Gironde area, and in the neighbourhood of Bordeaux, he and his cardinals built some seven castles. Villandraut is the most interesting of these, although not innovatory. It is a quadrangle castle, from which Bodiam could well have developed. Like the earlier works of Phillip Augustus, hoardings were preferred to machicolations. The walls were 29 metres (95 ft) high, with even taller corner towers, and were 6 metres (19.6 ft) thick at the battered base. The angles where the towers met the walls were filled with built out latrines, which could serve the more sinister purpose of machicolations in time of war. An identical feature can be seen in England, at Amberley in Sussex, an episcopal castle built in 1379. As befitted the dignity of a Pope, the interior of Villandraut must have been splendid, to judge by the ruined remains.

It was however, purely a private residence, and not suitable for a court.

Once it became clear that the Papacy was to become a permanency at Avignon, the desire was felt for a fitting establishment. The old bishop's palace was taken over and extended by subsequent Papal tenants – turning it into a fortress as well as an ecclesiastical centre. Benedict XII undertook a massive rebuild, adding the Pope's Tower in the late 1330s. He was also responsible for the prominent arched machicolation on the outer curtain, so similar to that originally used at Gaillard. Benedict's successor Clement VI, almost doubled the area of the palace, turning it into what Froissart described as the 'finest and strongest building in the world'.

The long period of peace preceding the Hundred Years War had caused many French castles to fall into decay. The eruption of English armies into the country was naturally the cause of much hasty refortifying. This included the adding of machicolation to many older structures, including the castles at Chambois, Montlhéry and the Phillip de Bel Tower at Villeneuve les Avignon. The latter was originally built to keep an eye on the Popes on the other side of the river. For the same purpose and in the same place, was one of the most satisfyingly designed of all the French castles – the Fort St. André, built 1362–68. This is not a particularly large work, and as a royal stronghold created for purely military purposes, foreshadowed the development of the artillery fort in the sixteenth century. Without any form of keep, it is simply a courtyard surrounded by massive walls, with the main defensive emphasis on the gate. The towers at the corners are the same height as the curtains, giving the effect of a massive solidarity, and the machicolated frieze is continued all around. The towers flanking the actual gateway feature loopholes at the base for true horizontal defence.

While in the area, there are two further castles on the Rhône worthy of mention – Tarascon and Beaucaire, standing opposite each other on the banks of the river. The former was a royal building dating from around 1400. It is the normal quadrangular work, and opposed to its hospitable interior, has a distinctly military exterior. Again, the corner towers are flush with the tops of the walls to form a fighting platform. Beaucaire features a unique triangular donjon dating from the twelfth century. This was raised in the fourteenth century, when the typical corbelled machicolation was added.

We in England tend to think of the Hundred Years War in terms of the glorious victories of Crecy, Poitiers and Agincourt, helped in many ways by the imagination of William Shakespeare. In fact, the war was mainly a brutal and messy affair. Large parts of France were literally laid waste by the ravages of the so-called Free Companies – roving mercenary bands. This led to a situation similar to that on the Scottish border, with the minor nobility fortifying their manors by adding towers. Sieges were numerous, both of walled castles and towns, and as the war ground on, chivalry tended to disappear, to be replaced by sheer butchery – of townsfolk and defeated garrisons alike. Plunder was the order of the day, and formed the basis of the financial wherewithal for so many English castles of the fourteenth and early fifteenth centuries.

The threat of an English siege led to a comprehensive refortification of Paris during the latter part of the fourteenth century – initiated after the French defeat at Poitiers in 1536. The Louvre ended up inside the new enceinte of Charles V, and thus lost its military importance as the main citadel. It became transformed into a residence, and was replaced by the Bastille, which was finally finished in 1382. This was a large and impressive rectangular work flanked by eight towers on battered plinths. The exterior was totally devoid of windows or decoration, and the flush towers and walls were surmounted by a machicolated gallery all round. After the French Revolution in later years, not a stone of the Bastille was left, such was the hatred felt by the population of the city for what was, for them, a blatant symbol of oppression.

The concept of the tower house appears at Vincennes, close to Paris, also initiated by Charles V as a royal stronghold. The centrepiece of the castle was a massive tower donjon some 60 metres (197 ft) high, constructed in the 1360s. It was surrounded by a chemise wall and a ditch to separate it entirely from the bailey which served as a fortified camp with its own flanked enceinte. It would seem that the troops of the French king were just as unreliable as those of the English monarch. It resembles in many ways the much older Tower of the Temple in Paris, once the headquarters of the Order of the Templars until they were dissolved by Phillippe le Bel in 1307. It is clear that the keep at Vincennes was designed as a royal abode, rising altogether through six storeys. An interesting feature is that the topmost floor was set back from the line of the allure, so as to command it if it should be occupied by an enemy. The main enceinte has Roman overtones like the camp at Aigues Mortes. It was flanked by nine rectangular towers, most of which were subsequently cut down to wall level. Originally they were some 30 metres (98.4 ft) high with vaulted roofs to take the shock of the engines mounted on them.

Pierrefonds is one of the last of the French castles with any potential for defensive capability. It was built around 1400 by Louis of Orleans, the brother of Charles VI, and rather fancifully restored by Viollet le Duc for Napoleon III. The outside walls are enormously high and almost blank, until a machicolated gallery is reached. Above this is a separate wall-walk, commanded in its turn by the roofs of the uppermost storey. The whole of the skyline is a riot of roofs, turrets and crenellations. Inside, the apartments were magnificent, although there was provision for a separate keep tower for the owner. It is quite clear from the scale of the lower part of the walls that the place was intended to be defended if required.

In the fifteenth century the split between defence and residence became steadily more accentuated. At a lower level, the fortified manor house showed signs of a desire for embellishment, with the addition of the small *eschaugette* turrets that one also sees in Scottish tower houses of the period. Under the impact of artillery, castles like Langeais with their high walls and machicolation (1465) were becoming obsolete – it was in fact, never finished. Plessis Bourré, finished around 1472 featured high walls on only one side, and that only to provide floors for residential accommodation. The other three wings and the corner towers were brought down to the level of the first floor, and a wide moat was relied on for protection. Only the main tower at the south-east corner was machicolated, and the adjoining curtain featured a number of near vertical chutes cut into the parapet to launch projectiles on to the heads of attackers.

Bonaguil is said by a French authority to have been the last of the fortified castles in that country (1482–1530). The first stage was traditional, with the building of machicolated towers. In front however, a deep ditch was dug, and a low wall was built all around the complex, pierced with embrasures for horizontal gunfire. The west side featured a broad artillery platform for mounting heavy guns for counter-battery work. Thus it was a mixture of height, to guard against escalade, with low-level artillery defences. The writer would prefer however, to grant the distinction of being the last castle in France to Salses, built by a Spanish engineer in the 1490s. Its design was traditional insofar as it formed a rectangular walled enclosure with drum towers at each corner and a square donjon on one side. The towers were steeply scarped at the base, a

Fig. 10 Bonaguil Castle said to have been the last French fortified castle. (See also colour plates.)

device that was in use as an anti-mining precaution as far back as the end of the twelfth century. There however the similarity ends. For, instead of standing out proudly to confront its enemies, the whole castle was sunk into its ditch almost entirely below the level of the surrounding countryside. The parapets were curved to deflect shot, and the ditch was flanked by artillery mounted in casemates. Salses was, in fact, a mounting platform for artillery, and built at the time when a whole new chapter was to begin in the history of military architecture.

Like their English counterparts, however, the French nobility clung to military symbolism to embellish their country châteaux which replaced the castle as a living unit. Towers, turrets and machicolation still featured prominently in such works as Azay-le-Rideau and Chaumont. Mention should also be made of Josselin in Brittany, as an example of this flamboyant Gothic style. It was built by one of the Rohan family around 1500. The tower and the scarped wall still dominates the river front, but is surmounted by pinnacled dormer windows and extensive roofing.

In Spain, the feudal system never became permanently established, although until the Moors were finally expelled in 1492, there was an almost perpetual state of war in the 'Peninsular'. Thus the many castles built were used mainly as barracks for garrisons or as headquarters for the many orders of crusading knights. Although often built on older fortified sites, the great 'castles in Spain' were mainly products of the fifteenth and sixteenth centuries, demonstrating both French and Moslem influence. The famous Alhambra which dominates the town of Granada, started life as a simple hill fort in the ninth century, ending up as an enormous complex of palace cum fortress.

Many of the finest castles are in Castile, which evidently obtained its name from the many castles in the province. One of the most impressive is Coca, built in the late fifteenth century by the Bishop of Seville. Basically it is a concentric castle, but instead of the north European gatehouse, it features a corner keep. Built of brick, the walls are steeply battered, and the battlements are covered with rich Arab-inspired decoration. The castle of Fuensalda has a separate keep, bearing a remarkable affinity to that at Vincennes, with tall thin corner towers. Medina del Campo, one of the many works built by John II in the mid fifteenth century, has obvious French influence, in spite of being constructed in brick. Its round squat drum towers and machicolated frieze are typical of late fourteenth century French work, and it is concentric, in the sense of being a castle within a lower outer wall.

Portugal is likewise rich in castles. The Arab influence is particularly strong, with the emphasis on rectangular towers and regular shapes. A typical example is Almeira, built in the latter half of the fourteenth century by the Hospitallers. It is a simple quadrangle without machicolation. There are four corner towers, one of which is larger and forms an entrance keep. This comparatively simple inner bailey is surrounded by an unflanked outer enceinte to make the castle concentric. Although a beautifully clean design, its defensive capabilities would have been somewhat limited.

Fortress design in Germany during the later Middle Ages still continues to defy any logical attempt at classification. One cannot determine any particular style. In the last chapter it was said that the flanking principle was never resolutely applied there, partly on account of the inaccessible siting of many of the works, and that castles tended to grow as a confused group of buildings surrounded by a wall. This tendency continued with piecemeal additions to existing works, including some machicolation and the addition of hanging turrets. One example of a mini-castle stands out however, and that is the Pfalz at Kaub on the Rhine, featured in many examples of tourist literature. Blücher crossed the river at that point in 1814, en route for Paris. The Pfalz was built as a toll collecting station on a reef in the river, by the Archbishop of Trier in the early part of the fourteenth century. The ashlar base is in the shape of a ship, on which is mounted a quaintly roofed superstructure clustered around a tower. The same worthy archbishop was also responsible for the residential tower at Eltville, remarkably similar to such contemporary structures in England. Lacking strong central government and split into small units, there were few magnates in Germany rich enough to indulge in magnificent castle building. Germany however, was a centre of trans-European trade, with a growing concentration of power in the cities. General lawlessness forced these communities to spend money on their defences, as well as to act offensively at times, to destroy the castles of the robber knights who preyed on the merchants' caravans. Many fine examples of town walls have been preserved, and the classic place to visit is of course, Rothenburg ob der Tauber in Bavaria, a one time free Imperial city. Its defences date mainly from the thirteenth and fourteenth centuries, with the typical tall slender towers crowned by conical roofs. The wooden roofed *coursière* atop the allure of the curtains has been well re-constructed. Slightly later and more impressive is Nuernberg, with a double ring of walls adapted for defence against artillery. The gates to the inner city are dominated by massive sixteenth century artillery towers fronted by barbicans.

Although most of the German castles were built on naturally strong hilltop sites, where sophisticated defences were often unnecessary, there are one or two beautiful moated castles in low-lying parts of the country. Mespelbrunn, in the Spessart forest lies idyllically in the middle of a lake. It was here that Julius Echter was born, one of the sixteenth century Prince Bishops of Wuerzburg. There is a thirteenth century round tower keep, obviously part of an older work, surrounded by residential buildings of a composite gracefulness. Most of these *Wasserburgen* however, are to be found on the plains of northern Germany. Examples are Glücksburg, near Flensburg, and Gudenau. The latter, built in the fourteenth century, is a contemporary of Bodiam, and is also quadrangular with strong corner towers and an imposing flanked gatehouse; there, however, the similarity ends. Gudenau cannot be defended from the parapet, as this became part of the roof over the interior buildings. Also, the curtain was pierced by prominent windows. It is thus more akin to the much later Herstmonceaux.

The threat to central Europe at the time came from the East. In the thirteenth century the Mongol Tartars had swept through to Poland and Hungary, to be followed in turn by the Turks, who were to remain a menace to security until the eighteenth century. Thus Austria and Hungary are particularly rich in castles, especially along such natural lines of approach as the Danube valley. The area along the Austrian frontier with Hungary is still known today as the Burgenland, because of the number of castles there. Like Germany, hill-top sites were preferred, and no particular style evolved. In addition, many mediaeval works had artillery bastions tacked on in the sixteenth and seventeenth centuries. A regular castle is difficult to find, most of them having grown up around the original watch tower keep, which was often retained. These were underdeveloped countries in the Middle Ages, without the resources for massive building programmes on a French or English scale.

It is to Italy that we must turn in search of originality. The Italians have always been an ingenious people, and in the late Middle Ages, the component regions of the Italian peninsular were actively engaged in

Fig. 11   Coca Castle in Spain. Built in the fifteenth century.

trade. As in the German states, this commerce tended to merge culturally and socially in the form of the town. In fact, many of the later castles were placed within the confines of the towns; for example, the Castello d'Este in Ferrara and the Castello di Corte at Mantua. One of the reasons for this factor lay in chaotic conditions, whereby citizens were forced to place themselves under the protection of a powerful family, for defence against other similar predators. Inter family strife however, was also rampant within the towns. The high walls defended against the enemy without, while individual townsmen were forced to defend themselves against their immediate neighbours. The classical example of this can still be seen at San Gimignano, where the skyline is dominated by the slender private towers of various families once at war with each other. Bologna also still has one or two such towers standing. This is the Italy of Machiavelli and the Borgias, soon to become a battleground for greedy foreign potentates. A country full of every form of vice, trickery and corruption, but matched by unparalleled creative achievement in the arts.

The two previously mentioned town castles at Ferrara and Mantua are broadly speaking similar, both being quadrangular fortresses built by powerful noblemen. Being in towns, their approaches were severely restricted. The Este castle is in many ways typical of the late fourteenth century. The walls are high and flanked by rectangular towers. The machicolation is mounted on corbels joined by arches, and the merlons have swallow-tail tops, which still can be seen under the later masonry added to the top. Sirmione, on Lake Garda is a brick construction of the fifteenth century, but already an anachronism when it was built. Its silhouette is a riot of tall square towers with decorative crenellations, and one of its most original features is an attractive fortified dock enclosing part of the lake.

The state of anarchy attracted soldiers of fortune from all over Italy, bringing with them knowledge of all the latest techniques of warfare. After France proved no longer profitable as a hunting ground, Knollys, the English commander of the famous White Company, took his band into Italy where he hired it out to various factions. Artillery was soon in use, and the Italians returned to the round form of tower, building them low and squat to deflect projectiles. The bases were further defended by massive plinths, often extending more than half-way up the tower itself. The Italians were probably the first to realise the possibilities of heavy artillery for defensive rather than offensive purposes, which meant the end of the high tower and curtain. Mobility was necessary on the fighting platform, so they developed lower versions of such castles as Tarascon and the Bastille. A fine example is the Rocca, or fort, at Senigallia, which still however, features machicolations. One presumes that at this stage this was still intended for defensive purposes, although it lingered on for many years as a decoration. Similarly in the 1480s, the Rocca at Ostia was built as a pure artillery fort, but still had a tower in the centre. Embrasures were cut in the corner towers almost at ground level, from which the whole area of the ditch could be swept by fire.

The angle bastion, the stable component of artillery defence until the end of the eighteenth century, developed out of the round tower that was reduced in height to mount guns. In all parts of Europe where money was lacking to build new fortifications, bastions were tacked on to existing mediaeval castles, and high walls were padded with earth. In Germany today, for instance, there are several examples in Bavaria of hill-top castles which have been surrounded with baroque bastions on the slopes of the site below the original work. The Plassenburg at Kulmbach has the early round bastions, and Kronach and Eichstaett have angle bastions. The Marienfeste at Wuerzburg was first modified by a pair of bastions on the main land front, to flank the gate into the outer bailey. These however were still topped by wooden *coursières* for hand to hand fighting. Later in the early eighteenth century, the whole of the fortress complex was added to by enclosing it within a comprehensive system of bastions and outworks. The fortress of Salzburg, familiar to so many visitors is also an example of such modifications.

There were two alternative fates for obsolete castles; either to crumble into elegant decay, or to be converted by their owners into smart residences. In keeping with the centralist aims of many monarchies, those that might have posed some form of future threat were slighted. In England, the mediaeval castles enjoyed a brief swan-song, before capitulating to the Parliamentary artillery train during the Civil War. Many of them put up notable resistances, and of those which were defended and ultimately surrendered, many were demolished. Cromwell, who had his reasons, must surely rank as one of the greatest destroyers of mediaeval military architecture. His equivalent and contemporary in France was Cardinal Richelieu, who during the early part of the seventeenth century was busily establishing the French monarchy on an absolutist basis. To do this, the power of the nobility had to be broken for good, which meant wholesale demolition of their castles. At the same time in Germany, the Thirty Years War was raging, which accounted for the ruinous state of most of the castles there today. Those that survived that conflict fell victim to the eighteenth century wars or those of the Napoleonic period. Among the latter was Rheinfels, that had in the meanwhile become an artillery fortress.

7

THE ROMANTIC REVIVAL

The nineteenth century was to witness an enormous revival of interest in mediaeval history, which as far as architecture was concerned, was to bring out the best, and the worst, in the Victorians and their continental counterparts. This was an age of great wealth and the establishment of new families among the ruling classes, who, when they had made their money in the towns, tended to set themselves up as country gentry. And what better way to do this than by building themselves a castle? It is easy to laugh at beer-brewer gothic and municipal mediaeval, but it is apparent that those who paid for it were highly satisfied with the results, and thought that they were getting value for their money. Not only the nouveau-riches however were inspired by history. George IV commissioned Wyatt to rebuild Windsor, and in the course of the work, the Henry II shell keep was increased in size and topped with a machicolated frieze – a feature that still dominates the skyline of this very English castle.

The Romantic Movement started in Germany in the late eighteenth century, when the Rhine Valley was part of the obligatory grand tour for enlightened noblemen. In 1774, Goethe was there and wrote the ballad *Hoch auf dem Alten Turm*, which in turn inspired a flood of similar literature. Byron was also impressed by the Rhine, as evidenced in *Childe Harold*, and the river and its castles formed the background for Longfellow's *Golden Legend*. The poets however, tended to find their sources among the troubadours, with their tales of courtly love and knight errantry. Thus it was that a somewhat false picture of the romanticism of the Middle Ages was created, far removed from the reality. Sir Walter Scott made a fortune out of the Middle Ages, and Tennyson revived interest in the Arthurian legends, still insisting in retaining them in the time scale of the troubadour era. This early period is also noteworthy for follies and fake ruins. If you had the misfortune not to have a ruined castle on your land, you built yourself one. The

Loewenburg, near Kassel in Germany, is one such, built in the 1790s by the Elector Wilhelm I.

All over England, country mansions appeared decorated with battlements and towers, suitable for such personages as the Duke of Omnium. Drawbridges that were permanently fixed lead to imposing entrances from which the spikes of fake portcullises protruded threateningly. Scottish baronial and such similar manifestations were obviously purely decorative – designed to enhance the supposed antiquity of the owner's lineage. What is more interesting is that certain architects set out to create mediaeval castles from scratch – complete with modern plumbing. One of the early examples of such nineteenth century reproductions is Penrhyn Castle, designed by Thomas Hopper for Lord Penrhyn in 1827. This work features a magnificent neo-Norman rectangular keep, liberally provided with windows, however. Even more exotic was Anthony Salvin's Peckforton Castle, constructed for Lord Tollemache between 1846 and 1850. This was not a folly or a joke. It was a serious attempt to recreate a complete mediaeval castle, within which the noble lord could live a life of style.

More praiseworthy were the efforts of the early restorers. In 1875, the Marquess of Bute commissioned the architect William Burges to rebuild the ruined Castell Coch, near Cardiff. The result was a most pleasing re-creation of a small fourteenth century castle, although the conical roofs probably owed more to France than to England, and may well have been inspired by the works of Viollet le Duc – of whom mention has already been made in connexion with Carcassonne and Pierrefonds. It has become fashionable in some quarters to sneer at le Duc, who it must be admitted, did at times get carried away by his imagination. Without the efforts of such men however, to point the way, our knowledge of mediaeval military architecture would have been much the poorer.

The castle theme in England was not restricted to dwellings. It was used throughout the nineteenth century, especially in barracks and prisons. Several of the Victorian forts sported crenellations and brattices over the gateways. To those readers familiar with Oxford, the Crown Court building must surely rank as a classic of neo-mediaevalism gone wrong, with its nonsensical array of battlements, machicolations and arrow-loops. Even the child's fort has carried this symbolism on into our times, with its corner towers and crenellations, and the castle features boldly as an advertising theme for such solid foundations as banks and building societies.

The Germans were also busy with restorations, many of which were in doubtful style. Frederick William IV of Prussia rebuilt Stolzenfels on the Rhine in decorative neo-Gothic, setting a fashion. Many other ruins were bought up by imitators, made habitable and stuffed with suits of armour and heraldic decorations. In better taste was the work undertaken by Wilhelm II at Haut-Koenigsbourg in Alsace, in the early years of this century. This castle, at present in France, was rebuilt partly to emphasize the Germanic nature of the provinces annexed after 1870.

I have reserved for last, the man who must surely have been the most notable of the castle imitators. I refer to Ludwig II, King of Bavaria, a monarch who was felt by many to have been mad, but whose fantasies have given pleasure to millions of tourists since his day. Deeply fascinated by the old Germanic legends, and strongly under the not always benign influence of Wagner, he set out to surround himself with the trappings of his heroes. His first effort was the restoration of an earlier work, the castle of Hohenschwangau. Not satisfied with this, however, he decided to build something new in style, the result being Neuschwanstein, surely the supreme fairy tale castle. This castle has been used in Walt Disney films, and is a regular feature of German tourist advertising. It was begun in 1869 and was finished in 1886, with a number of architects involved. The result was a superb toy in an even more superb setting. Perched on top of a rock outcrop covered by trees, the castle looks down on an azure lake, with the Alps for a background. It was also the background for the tragic end of the King, on account of the enormous sums spent on the work. The Bavarian government had him declared mad, and he supposedly committed suicide by drowning, still a compellingly attractive figure in this somewhat drab age.

8

SIEGE WARFARE

So far we have traced the development of the castle as a structure. As its purpose however, was essentially military, we must turn to its rôle within the general history of warfare. This has naturally been touched on in previous chapters, but needs certain amplifications. We have seen that siege warfare was practised in the ancient world. The Romans refined the art to such an extent that their mediaeval imitators could hardly effect any improvements. Like warfare in the field, it was a question of attack and defence, but by the end of the thirteenth century the castle had become so strong that the advantage definitely lay with the latter. This is one of the reasons why warfare in the later Middle Ages tended to become more an affair of battles, and why so many of the great castles have little or no military history. The practicalities of besieging a fortified place were largely a matter of logic, thought out and improved upon by clever minds through the ages. Our primitive caveman who barricaded his lair, created an obstacle. His enemy, when confronted with this defensive feature, and perhaps after a painful repulse, was forced to retire and to think again. Two solutions would probably have occurred to him. Depending upon his need for haste, he could either attempt to surmount the barricade, or to sit and wait until hunger and thirst achieved the desired result. What follows is only refinement.

Stories of sieges abound in the ancient chronicles, but have to be treated with caution. The writers of such epics were mostly monks, who did not necessarily have any knowledge of the practicalities of warfare. Many of them were not eyewitness accounts, and no doubt to impress the readers, exaggeration was frequently resorted to for effect. Reports of numbers of men involved must normally be halved. Few of the thousands of sieges chronicled were formal attacks against large well-defended castles. By far the majority were muddled affairs involving a haphazard assault against a small ill-garrisoned work.

Having stated these qualifications, there remain certain basic methods of attacking a fortified place, which have not really changed over the centuries, and they are:

Escalade – the climbing of the obstacle.
Breaching the obstacle by battering or undermining.
Setting it on fire.
Starving out the garrison.
Treachery, bribery and assorted trickery.

Having already said that there was no such thing as an impregnable castle, one or other of the above methods was bound eventually to work – depending on the time and the resources available.

As the art of war is a logical progression, the weapons available to besiegers developed in a direct ratio to the strength of the places that they would be called upon to attack. On the other hand, castles developed in accordance with the weapons that were likely to be set against them. A full scale siege of a larger castle or well defended town called for enormous resources both in men and *matériel*. As it was likely to be a long drawn out affair, it could not be undertaken with a feudal army, but called for mercenary troops and the wherewithal to pay them. The use of siege machinery and mining called for specialists – artificers, carpenters, metal workers – who might have to be recruited from afar. The necessary building materials had to be either locally available, or transported to the site, a difficult undertaking in a period of poor communications. There are many occasions in history of a siege having to be abandoned through lack of resources.

The motte and bailey castle satisfied the basic need for protection in the eleventh century. The basis of its defence was a wooden palisade, that still proved effective against Red Indians armed with rifles in the nineteenth century. When fronted by a ditch and stiffened by thorn bushes, the mediaeval equivalent of barbed wire, it rendered the mounted knight useless. Although western armies had some knowledge of stone throwing engines at the time, they were not generally used until the advent of the stone castle. The attack of such a castle might progress on the lines of the following reconstruction based on Archbishop Suger's account of an attack made by Louis VI on the castle of Le Puiset in 1111.

After the defenders had been driven inside the castle, an attempt was made to storm the gatehouse of the bailey, and then to set it alight. Carts

Archer drawing his bow

Archer

Crossbow-man

Crossbow-man tensioning
his weapon

Fig. 12   Long bow and crossbow.

full of wood soaked in fat were pushed up, under a storm of missiles hurled by the garrison. The defenders managed to extinguish the burning carts, and they likewise repulsed an assault across the ditch and up the rampart. Finally however, a breach in the palisade was made, forcing the garrison to retreat into the tower on the motte, where they shortly afterwards surrendered. This was a fairly brief siege, characterized by hand to hand combat.

The weapons available to both sides were spears, bows, swords and axes. In connexion with bows, we are not talking incidentally about the Welsh longbow. That only came into general use in the early part of the fourteenth century. Owing to its size, it was unsuitable for use in the defence of a castle anyway. Early mediaeval bowmen were of two kinds; those using the short stringed bow, and those using the crossbow. This latter weapon was known to the Romans, and one unproven source states that William the Conqueror's army used them at Hastings. The Crusaders who arrived at Constantinople on the First Crusade in 1096. certainly possessed them, but they were unknown to the Byzantines according to Anna Comnena. She describes the crossbow as a weapon of war which had to be stretched lying almost on one's back. The feet were pressed against the bow while the string was tugged back towards the body. In the middle of the string was a groove into which short, thick, iron-tipped arrows were fitted. On discharge, such arrows could transfix a shield, cut through a heavy iron breastplate and resume their flight on the other side. This may have been an exaggeration, but the crossbow certainly had immense hitting power. Later versions were developed whereby the string could be tensioned by levers or ratchets, making them available to even the weakest member of the garrison. An interesting fact is that at the Lateran Council in 1139, they were banned as inhuman weapons – a ban which obviously did not have the slightest effect. Its defects were a slow rate of fire, and the cost of the bolts that it fired.

Let us now consider the basic siege methods in connexion with an attack on a stone castle, from the point of view of theory. The first duty of the attacking commander was to ensure that he had enough troops to adequately surround the place, to prevent supplies being carried to the garrison inside. If there was a chance that a relieving force could arrive on the scene, he would then have to fortify his own camp by digging lines of ditch and ramparts all around it – facing the object under siege to hinder sallies by the garrison, and facing the open country to defend against a

1   Castell St. Angelo, Rome.

2   The Roman Walls of Portchester Castle, Hampshire.

3   Part of the Aurelian Wall, Rome.

4   Loches, France, The Angevin donjon.

5　The motte at Bramber in Sussex.

6　Turkey. Near Lake Van.

7   Tower of London. The White Tower.

8   Restormel Castle, Cornwall, The shell keep.

9   Lewes Castle, Sussex. Shell keep and flanking tower.

10 Portchester Castle. The keep and barbican.

11 Farnham Castle, Surrey. Wall of shell keep.

12   Rochester Castle, Kent. The great keep.

13   Castle Rising, Norfolk. The keep and earthworks.

14   The keep of Norham Castle, Northumberland.

15   Orford Castle, Suffolk. The early transitional keep.

16   Avila, Spain.

17 Dover Castle, Kent.

18 Falaise Castle, Normandy. On the left the Talbot Tower.

19   S'Gravensteen, Ghent, Belgium.

20   Niort, France. The   21   Vianden, Luxembourg.
double donjon.   Castle complex.

22 Krak des Chevaliers, Syria. The greatest of the Crusader castles.

23 The Crusader castle at Sidon in the Lebanon.

24 The Jerusalem
citadel by night.

25 Kokorin,
Czechoslovakia.

26 Kerak in Moab, Jordan.

27 Pernstejn, Czechoslovakia.

28 Friars Castle, Spain.

29 Angers, Loire. Drum towers and postern gate.

30 The walls of Aigues Mortes, France.

31 Another view of Aigues Mortes.

32   Tour de Constance, Aigues Mortes.

33   Rosito Castle, Italy.

34 Castel Nuovo, Naples.

35 Castel del Monte, Apulia.

36 Knepp Castle, Sussex.

37 Bramber gatehouse keep.

38 Pevensey Castle. Interior stairway.

39 Pevensey Castle, Sussex. Norman towers and ditch.

40   The gateway to Framlingham Castle, Suffolk.

41   The Muiderslot Castle in the Netherlands.

42   Parts of the enceinte of Carcassonne in France.

43 The barbican at Lewes Castle in Sussex.

44 Carcassonne. The Porte Narbonnaise with barbican.

45 Another view of the walls of Carcassonne.

46 Amberley Castle, Sussex. The gatehouse.

47   Rhuddlan Castle, Wales.

48 The concentric arrangement of the Tower of London.

49 The Porte Gargoyle at Boulógne, France.

50   Conway Castle, Wale

51   Caerphilly Castle, Wale

52   Harlech Castle, Wales. Another concentric example.

53 Beaumaris Castle, Wales.

54 Postern gate, Beaumaris.

55 Part of the enceinte, Beaumaris

56 Kidwelly Castle, Wales.

57 Caernarvon Castle, Wales. The Eagle Tower.

58　Goodrich Castle, Welsh border.

59　Bodiam Castle, Sussex.

60 Lucens Castle,
    Switzerland.

61 Spiez Castle,
    Switzerland.

62 Burg Stahleck
above
Bacharach,
Rhineland.

63 Marienberg
Castle,
Wuerzburg,
Germany.

64 The keep at
Kenilworth
Castle in
Warwickshire.

65 Manorbier
Castle, Wales.

66 Warwick Castle
and the River
Avon.

67 The Vicar's
Pele, Corbridge,
Northumberland.

68   Herstmonceaux Castle, Sussex. The main gate.

69 Oravsky Podzamok, Czechoslovakia.

70 The Fort St. André at Villeneuve-les-Avignon.

71   The Papal Palace at Avignon.

72 The donjon at
Beaucaire.

73 Another view of the
Beaucaire donjon.

74 The fourteenth century castle at
Tarascon.

75 The Tower of Phillip,
Villeneuve-les-Avignon.

76 Fougères Castle on the Brittany frontier.

77 Vitré, another of the Brittany frontier works.

78 Château de
L'Hers, France.

79 Château
Josselin,
Brittany.

80 Saumur on the Loire.

81 Bonaguil. Sally port.

82 Bonaguil. Fireplace.

83 Bonaguil. Loophole.

84 Bonaguil. Stairway.

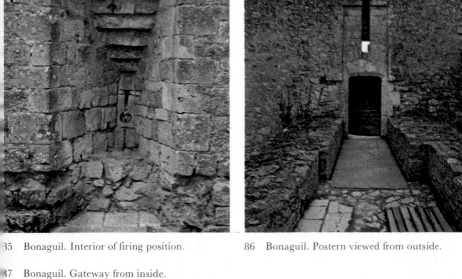

85 Bonaguil. Interior of firing position.

86 Bonaguil. Postern viewed from outside.

87 Bonaguil. Gateway from inside.

88   Azay-le-Rideau on the Loire.

89 Bonaguil Castle, France.

90 Donnington Castle, Berkshire, Gatehouse.

91 Salses in Rousillon, France. Note the curved parapets.

92 Consuegra Castle, Toledo, Spain.

93 Penafiel Castle, Spain.

94 La Calahorra Castle, Granada, Spain.

95 Valencia
Castle,
Spain.

96 Fuensalda Castle, Spain.

97 Orgaz Castle, Spain.

98   Mendoza Tower, Alana, Spain.

99   Manzaneres el Real, Madrid Province, Spain.

100   La Mota Castle, Spain.

104 Wolframs
Eschenbach, Bavaria.

105 Front view of
Langeais, France.

106 The interior of a
barbican at Amberg
in Bavaria.

107   The Marienberg fortress at Wuerzburg.

108   Inoux Castle in the Pyrenees.

109　Windsor
　　Castle,
　　Berkshire,
　　England.

110　Castello di S. Zeno and town walls at Montagnana, Italy.

111   Senigallia Rocca, Italy.

112   The Rocca at Ostia, Italy.

113   The restored profile of Arundel Castle, Sussex.

114   The Rocca at Forli, Italy.

115   The spectacular silhouette of Sirmione Castle on Lake Garda.

116   Konopiste, central Czechoslovakia.

117   A part of Haute-Koenigsbourg in Alsace.

118   Stolzenfels Castle on the Rhine.

119   Castell Coch, near Cardiff, Wales.

120   Liechtenstein Castle.

121 Neuschwanstein Castle, Bavaria.

relieving field army. If such help did come to the assistance of their comrades in the castle, the original attacker might find himself with the rôles reversed, being besieged in his own entrenched camp. Of the methods of attack that we listed, escalade was the quickest and simplest, but attended by the greatest risks as far as troop losses were concerned. The scaling ladder thrown up against the wall could easily be thrown down, and heads and fingers appearing on the parapet could quickly be lopped off. In addition, the intrepid climbers on the way up would have been subject to all the frightful things that could be thrown down on them – boiling liquids, quicklime, iron bars, rocks and red-hot sand. The latter was evidently most effective against attackers wearing armour or chain-mail – it got inside the joints and made life uncomfortable. For those who fell off and landed in the ditch there was no mercy. There is one tale of an unfortunate knight in this position who had brushwood dropped on to him that was then set alight, roasting him alive in the oven of his armour. Escalade was most effective as a surprise night attack, or against a lightly held part of the defences, in conjunction with a diversionary assault perhaps.

The more sophisticated way to achieve the same ends – occupation of the wall-walk – was to use a so-called belfry. This was a massive wheeled tower, preferably higher than the wall to be attacked, which, when the ditch had been filled with rubble, was pushed up against the curtain. These were built up on a wooden framework with ladders inside leading to the fighting level – which would normally have a drawbridge to drop on to the parapet at the moment of assault. On top might be a crenellated roof filled with archers, to keep down the heads of the garrison. The whole structure would be covered by wet hides, to make it as fireproof as possible. Often such devices would house a battering-ram in the base which would simultaneously be working away to dislodge the masonry.

The siege tower however, was not necessarily used for a direct assault on the walls. Sometimes they were built close to the castle under siege as a form of counter-castle, either to guard the attackers's camp, or to sweep the area with fire from crossbowmen on the roof. There are even instances of such structures being made strong enough to mount stone-throwing engines on the top deck. Such counter-castles were sometimes referred to as *malvoisins* – bad neighbours.

Belfreys suffered from the disadvantage of weight and the afore-mentioned vulnerability to fire. They had to be constructed on site by competent workmen, and the filling of the ditch had to be solid enough to bear the enormous weight. Chronicles however, are full of instances of their employment. As early as 1096, Anna Comnena tells us that Raymond of Saint-Gilles built one during the siege of Nicaea – 'a wooden tower, circular in shape; inside and out he covered it with leather hides and filled the centre with intertwined wickerwork'. At the siege of Dyrrachium in 1108, Bohemond built a four-sided tower on a wooden base that was high enough to dominate the towers of the city. It was pushed forward on rollers by soldiers inside who levered it up – so that it was apparently 'self-propelled'. The many storeys had embrasures all around from which showers of arrows could be fired.

At the same time as towers were being built, the battering rams would be busy, probably the oldest method of breaking down a wall. It was basically a tree trunk with a metal head, and a variation was the bore, tipped with a metal spike. Now it was obvious that a crowd of men could not simply walk up to the wall and start battering away at it. They had to be protected, so a penthouse or cat was constructed. This was like a long shed on rollers or wheels, from the roof timbers of which the ram could be slung on chains. Inside, anything up to a hundred men would swing the ram to and fro. The penthouse had a steeply pitched roof to deflect projectiles, and had to be fireproofed with hides or metal plates. Like the belfry, the cat depended upon a well filled ditch as a base, and some accounts state that when in place the wheels were removed, to give a more solid foundation for the swinging movement.

Such penthouses were not necessarily purely for housing rams. Sometimes they were for sheltering miners, and Joinville describes similar structures built by the engineers of St. Louis to shelter troops who were making a causeway across the Nile, in 1249. These were protected at each end by wooden towers to act as guardhouses. Temporary wooden siege buildings also took to the water on occasions. In 1218, the participants in the Fifth Crusade were besieging Damietta at the mouth of the Nile. They were held up by a tower in the middle of the river, and a priest, Oliver of Paderborn, who wrote the account of the Crusade, designed a floating belfry. This was mounted on boats and floated down on to the tower, which it succeeded in overcoming.

While the battering rams were trying to effect a breach, a hail of missiles would be flying through the air, propelled by various forms of throwing machine. Although mainly restricted to the attacking forces,

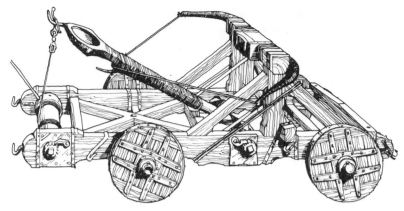

Fig. 13   Stone-throwing engine.

such devices were on occasions mounted by the defenders. Their use however, presupposed a really solid foundation, and vibration could do as much damage to walls and towers, as all the efforts of the enemy. Siege artillery came in three basic forms. The chronicles abound in fanciful names for them, but the collective term was *petrarii* – stone throwers. The forerunner of the modern howitzer or mortar was the mangonel, worked by torsion. Two stout posts were mounted on a firm chassis, and joined by skeins of rope. Between these a beam would be placed, with a hollowed out spoon-shaped depression at the throwing end. Into this a stone, or perhaps a fire pot would be inserted; the ropes would be twisted by a windlass to create torsion, and then suddenly released. This would cause the beam to rise smartly, propelling its load in a high curved trajectory. Other samples of ammunition used were dead horses and the severed heads of prisoners (bacteriological and psychological warfare!). Such weapons were not very accurate, and were best employed for bombarding the interior buildings of a castle – spreading alarm and confusion.

The second type of engine used tension as the propellant power. Known as a ballista, it was similar to a large crossbow and worked on the same principle. As in the case of the chicken and the egg conundrum, however, the ballista came first while the crossbow was a later development. Like the mangonel, it originated with the Greeks, and its employment at the siege of Rome in 537 AD was described thus by Procopius – 'These machines have the general shape of a bow, but in the middle is a hollow piece of horn fixed loosely to the bow, and lying over a straight stock. When wishing to fire at the enemy, you pull back the short strong cord that joins the arms of the bow, and place in the horn a bolt, four times as thick as the ordinary arrow, but furnished with wooden projections exactly reproducing the shape of the feathers. Men standing on either side of the weapon draw back the cord with winches. When they let it go, the horn rushes forward and discharges the bolt'. Later he states that he saw a mailed Goth impaled to a tree by a bolt from a ballista. At the siege of Paris in 885–6 AD, the monk Abbo tells us a likely tale. He says that he saw a bolt go through three Danes all at once, leaving them like chickens on a spit. Abbot Ebolus, obviously a skilled member of the church militant, who had fired it, called down to his comrades that they should pick the Danes up and take them to the kitchen. The ballista had a flat trajectory, and was reasonably accurate as it could be aimed by traversing the carriage. Its main use was as an anti-personnel weapon, although there were stone throwing versions.

One of the few innovations of the Middle Ages as far as siege warfare was concerned, was the trébuchet. In simple terms, it was a giant sling,

Fig. 14   Engine for shooting javelins.

164

and was worked by dropping a counterweight on the end of a throwing beam. It too was a howitzer type weapon but its accuracy was greater than the mangonel, as the range could be adjusted by moving the weight along the arm.

None of these primitive artillery weapons were really effective against a solidly built wall. The only way to effect a breach was to keep on battering away at the same point, for which absolute accuracy was necessary. Even in the eighteenth century, besiegers had to get their gun batteries on to the covered way, and bombard the escarp with hundreds

Fig. 15   Trébuchet or slinging machine.

of rounds before being able to demolish enough of it to fill the ditch, and they were using iron cannon balls. The only sure way of bringing down a wall, given that it could be approached and was not built on solid rock, was to undermine it. This however took time, and could not be undertaken by an attacker in a hurry. The technique was to excavate a cavity under a part of the enceinte, preferably at the angle of a tower. This would be shored up with timber props and filled with combustibles – we have already noted the use of fat pigs at Rochester in 1216. In theory the props would be consumed on firing and the masonry above would come crashing down – amid shouts of derision from the attackers. Mining was not then new. Herodotus describes identical techniques in use at the siege of Barca in 510 BC. It became much more difficult however, after the introduction of round towers and plinths. The garrison of a castle under siege, if they detected mining, could countermine by digging their own tunnel to break in on the enemy excavators. Having done this, they could drive them out by hand to hand combat with their shovels, or try to flood them out with water. Smoke was also a favourite device – as long as the wind was blowing in the right direction.

The use of fire was often resorted to by both sides during a siege. From the attackers' point of view, many of the parts of a castle were made of wood – especially the buildings in the bailey. As these often housed provisions and other stores, their destruction would reduce the capacity of a place to resist. Hoardings also were vulnerable, unless protected by hides. The defenders, for their part, would try to ignite the besiegers' equipment, either by throwing burning material or by sallying out on horseback. We do not have the exact recipe for Greek Fire, a substance that is often mentioned in the chronicles. It was apparently a Byzantine invention to judge from the name. Its components were probably a combination of such substances as naptha, pitch, resin and sulphur, and it could evidently be made to stick to the target. As a liquid, it could also be discharged through tubes, where it was a particularly potent weapon in naval warfare. At any rate, it must have been extremely unpleasant to be on the receiving end of such mediaeval napalm. One of the pictures of the Bayeux Tapestry shows two men trying to set fire to the wooden stockade of the motte and bailey castle at Dinant.

Starvation was a method reserved for attackers who had time, which as far as mediaeval armies were concerned, was a precious commodity. If the *castellan* of the castle being besieged had done his job properly, he would have stocked adequate provisions. The attacker had to have sufficient men to completely blockade the garrison, and be in a position not only to pay them, but to provision them as well. Otherwise he might himself be forced to raise the siege through starvation. In those days there were no organised commisssariat departments, and armies consumed what they could either buy or steal on the spot. When in inhospitable country, it proved extremely difficult to keep an army together. Foraging parties had to move far out, and such detachments meant a reduction in the blockading forces. More often than not, the besieging army melted away long before their enemy had been forced to capitulate.

If a quick decision was needed, and all assaults had failed, the last possibility was bribery or trickery. The latter was a favourite way of gaining entry, and there were always bold men willing to risk all on a slim chance. There were instances of armed men being smuggled into a castle hidden in fodder carts – before actual hostilities had begun. Once through the gate, they leapt out and overpowered the guard, opened the doors and let in their comrades. Forgery, too, was used. At the final siege of Krak des Chevaliers, the Moslems succeeded in penetrating the outer bailey, but were held up by the inner defences. They then showed the *castellan* a letter purporting to have come from the Grand Master of his Order, commanding him to surrender, as he could not be relieved. The *castellan* accepted this, and marched out with his men on being granted honourable terms – only to find out later that the letter was a fake.

Bribery too was often successful. The mediaeval soldier had his price, but was certainly not more or less venal than his modern counterpart. Throughout history there have been those willing to sell out a position of trust. In 1097, the Crusaders besieged Antioch for 6 months without success. One of their leaders however, Bohemond, managed to persuade the Moslem commander of one of the towers of the city to admit a troop of his men. They were let in at night, and made themselves masters of the wall, whereby the city capitulated. In this case, money was obviously more important than religion.

Anyone who has studied mediaeval history will have remarked how often a *castellan* could be persuaded to accept a bribe or to change allegiance. Before condemning such conduct out of hand, we have to forget twentieth century ideals of patriotism and bravery. 'God for Harry, England and St George', was a Tudor notion, put into the mouth of Henry V by William Shakespeare. In the Middle Ages, a man's loyalty was to his liege lord, his superior in the feudal pyramid, and not to vague concepts like 'France' or 'England'. The overall authority of a king was valid insofar as it could be enforced, and like most primitive societies, respect was granted to the powerful. Only those who ruled weakly were subject to rebellion and deposition. As there was no recognition of nation, it follows that treason could not exist, in the later sense of the word. The feudal oath carried with it obligations for both parties. If a man's lord broke his part of the bargain, his vassal was entitled to rebel. Thus a *castellan* of a castle could claim that he was justified in surrendering his charge, if his lord failed to come to his aid within a reasonable time – this was a frequent source of agreement between besieged and besieger. Much mediaeval strife was about points of personal honour, and such questions could only be resolved by battle according to the accepted customs of the time. Many mediaeval writers were shocked by the havoc caused by warfare, but did not condemn warfare as such. As an example, after John had failed to relieve Château Gaillard, most of the other castles in Normandy tamely surrendered to the French king – by not coming to the aid of the beleaguered Duchy, John had broken his feudal obligation to protect his vassals and thus forfeited their allegiance.

Much work remains to be done on the subject of the rules of mediaeval warfare. As earlier stated, the nobility of Europe formed an international caste, one of whose main occupations was warfare. In certain cases of private quarrels, hatred might turn into mutual slaughter, but generally speaking it made no sense to slaughter your opponent, when you could earn money by ransoming him, as long as he belonged to the upper classes. This principle did not apply to the foot soldiers, who were fair game. As far as siege warfare was concerned, once a castellan had put up a decent show of resistance, and could surrender with his honour intact, he could be sure of honourable confinement until ransomed. If, however, resistance was prolonged to the bitter end, and tempers became inflamed, the garrison might well be put to the sword when the place was finally taken. In the case of a town, the citizens were particularly vulnerable to plunder, rape and butchery, while the knights of the garrison could well be spared.

So far we have mainly spoken in terms of the attack. The *castellan* or constable of a castle however, when a siege threatened, had great responsibility. If he was conscientious, there were a number of tasks that had to be performed before hostilities began. All the able bodied men in the district had to be recruited, especially those with a feudal obligation to defend the castle. Then, provisions had to be gathered in, and the surrounding country as far as possible denuded of anything that could help the enemy to subsist. Nearby trees had to be cut down to deny their use to the enemy for shelter – besides which, the garrison would need stocks of timber for making running repairs. Non-combatants had to be expelled, as being useless mouths to feed. The whole place would have been alive with noise; the carpenters busy rigging the hoardings and repairing any weaknesses that had been ignored in peace-time; the armourers attending to the weapons that had become neglected and rusty for lack of use. Scouting parties sent out to gain intelligence or to burn standing crops for miles around would be clattering in and out. Other men would be carrying stocks of missiles up to the wall-walk and into the towers – stones, arrows, buckets of pitch and sand. Water had to be readily available for fire-fighting purposes. Press-ganged peasants might be clearing the ditch of brushwood, or throwing up earth entrenchments.

When the final warning came and the enemy was sighted, the bridge was raised and the doors fastened. The garrison hurried to man the walls and to size up their adversary, who would be greeted perhaps with catcalls and shouts of derision. Those inside, it must be remembered, were defending what was their home and thus had a vested interest in preserving it. From then on, the siege took its course.

One of the great mediaeval sieges, and one that is well documented, is that of Château Gaillard in Normandy in 1203-4. The story has often been told, but I make no apology for repeating it, because it represents an example of some of the best and some of the worst aspects of mediaeval warfare. The actual castle has already been described, and its attack was the result of enmity between King John of England and Phillip Augustus, the King of France. King John had done away with Arthur, the son of his late elder brother, and Phillip as a means of fomenting strife had espoused Arthur's cause. The advent of a French army in Normandy sent John hurrying back to England from his Norman possessions, and in August 1203, Phillip arrived in front of the castle. The story of the siege comes from the chronicler Guillaume le Breton. The constable of the castle was Roger de Lacy, a member of one of the foremost Anglo-Norman families. After one relief attempt had failed, de Lacy must have realised that there would be a fight to the finish. Phillip's mercenary army first tried to capture the bridge across the Seine at Les Andelys, which became the scene of bitter fighting. Guillaume lovingly recounts the grisly details of the injuries sustained. This is the real stuff of mediaeval warfare – severed limbs and heads, gushing blood and entrails, axes, clubs and swords doing their deadly work. Screams and curses as pitch was poured down on those fighting below. Death was a release for the lucky ones. For the injured, who might lie for days without attention, survival meant a few more years as a cripple, ekeing out an existence by begging.

After being repulsed at the bridge, a swimmer got across carrying a sealed pot of hot coals. With this he managed to fire the wooden stockade around the township of Les Andelys, which resulted in the whole place burning down. The unfortunate inhabitants fled into the castle carrying what they could, while the French King set down to form a close blockade. De Lacy expelled a group of these useless inhabitants, who were permitted to pass through the besiegers' lines, but when he threw out another group, they were trapped between the castle and the French, who tried to drive them back in to encourage eventual starvation by helping to consume food. They found however, the gates barred against them, and were soon reduced to desperate straits – there is even a mention of cannibalism. It was the French king who finally took pity on the wretches, and let them go. There is a similar instance at the siege of Calais by Edward III in 1346. There a group of non-combatants starved to death between the two armies.

The blockade went on for 6 months, lasting until the spring. Phillip must have realised that he could wait no longer, for he decided to open the attack. There was only one way to assault Gaillard, and that was the hard way, taking it bailey by bailey. Operations were commenced against the triangular outwork, with the levelling of the ground and bringing up materials to fill the ditch. Catapults and siege towers were constructed on site, and hurried into action. Both sides employed picked marksmen. Success however went to the miners, who hollowed out a large enough cavity to bring down the wall in a cloud of smoke and dust. 'Round one' to the King of France, as the defenders retreated into the middle bailey, burning everything behind them. The middle bailey was a much tougher proposition, but at this stage as happens so often in warfare, luck intervened.

A small group of Phillip's soldiers went prowling around on the steep slopes to the west of the castle, no doubt up to no good. There they espied a window that led into the crypt of the chapel, and which they managed to reach by creeping up a latrine shaft. Once inside they set up an enormous clamour, and in the ensuing confusion, managed to get to the drawbridge and let it down. It is possible that the sight of the latrine crawlers, and the smell, put the defenders to flight. Anyway, the French rushed in while the garrison fled into the inner bailey. The paradox is that it was John who had added the chapel, and had thus introduced a weakness into Richard's original design.

Siege engines made no impression on the walls of the inner bailey, with their odd scalloped design. There was however, a lump of rock which afforded shelter to a group of miners. Admittedly they were dislodged by the garrison, but their activities had so weakened the wall above that it finally collapsed. At this stage there was a scramble for the breach. The garrison made no attempt to retreat into the donjon, which in fairness, may not have been finished at the time. Instead, they tried to retire through the postern, but were soon rounded up by the French. They must have realised by then that they no longer stood a chance, either of holding out or being relieved. A last stand in the donjon would have been a futile gesture.

Thus ended the siege of Gaillard, in many ways typical of a serious attack on a strong castle by a well-equipped enemy. Most of the accepted methods of both defence and attack were used, by garrison and attackers. An element of chance was introduced into the proceedings, but the castle need not have fallen if adequate steps had been taken for its relief. The present ruinous state of the castle is not though a result of the siege. Immediately afterwards, it was repaired by the French, and saw action several times during the Hundred Years War. Its final slighting was ordered by Richelieu at the beginning of the seventeenth century.

9
THE CASTLE IN PEACE-TIME

One cannot get away with studying castles purely from the point of view of their rôle in war. For most of their time they lived at peace, although in a state of readiness for action if required. It is a mistake to assume that a castle was permanently packed with armed men, and that the battlements bristled with brandished weapons. Most of them were occupied by a minimal garrison for most of the time, which would be reinforced by feudatories when required. The day to day aspect of the castle is the one that has been the least researched so far, and the many books on mediaeval 'life' have only scratched the surface. The available evidence is in many ways unreliable, consisting as it does of chronicles and the illustrations from manuscripts. What follows therefore, is basically a number of generalisations, strictly limited by the space available.

The time span of this book covers several centuries, during which great changes occurred in the life-styles of the upper classes, which we have already seen reflected in the development of their dwellings. When the Normans came to England in 1066, they inherited a reasonably well-organised administration, that continued to function under the new masters. Actual government was centred in the person of the king – where he went, the administration went too. In the early days, the treasury was a box under the king's bed. Because of poor communications, the court, in order to govern, had to travel constantly. In addition, the king found it easier to progress from manor to manor, eating the available provisions, rather than having them transported to some central place. A tradition of spending the great feasts of the year at pre-ordained places prospered, at venues such as Winchester, Westminster and Woodstock. There, the king wore his crown of state and received his barons. Justice was at first vested in the barons, but during the reign of Henry II, more and more judicial functions were performed by the crown. The sheriffs of the counties were royal officials, and in addition, cases were heard by travelling judges on circuit – who would have held court in the halls of the royal castles. Around the person of the king, a group of officers of state emerged, who originally performed menial functions – hence their titles of butler, chamberlain, steward etc. In course of time, these became hereditary positions of responsibility while still bearing their lowly names.

A baron's court was in many ways a miniature version of the king's. He, too, had to travel to administer his often scattered demesne, and to supervise his bailiffs and other local servants. With him he would have a retinue of his personal followers, their number depending upon his ability to maintain them. A large retinue was a status symbol. Behind the mounted followers, who would while away the journey by hunting and hawking, would come the baggage train, attended by the menials. A long line of pack animals would transport such items as the lord's bed and the hangings for his bedchamber, cooking utensils and furniture. It was usual to have only one set of such things that would be carried around from castle to castle.

The motte and bailey castle was a primitive affair, and it is obvious that the normal tower house on the mound would only have served as a place of refuge. The house described by Lambert of Ardres must have been an exception. The basic living unit of the old Germanic tribes was the hall or longhouse. The Anglo-Saxons lived in such dwellings, and the palace at Bosham owned by Harold, was, according to the Bayeux Tapestry, a two-storeyed affair. The ground floor was a vaulted storage space, and the first floor, reached by an external staircase, was one large room. Similar buildings would have been constructed of wood, in the baileys of the earlier castles. In them, the garrison would have eaten, entertained themselves and slept. The first floor of a rectangular keep fulfilled initially a similar function.

In the twelfth century, we note that with the rise of the stone castle and the strong curtain, the separate hall appears, usually built against one of the walls. In its simplest form, it was again a two-storey building, with storage underneath. This was particularly important, in that a castle needed adequate space to stock up in case of siege. On top would be the basic hall room, with an entrance via a stairway at one end. It would have been divided into three parts, a division that can still be seen in the dining halls of many Oxbridge colleges today. First came the servery, partitioned off from the rest by a wooden screen. This did not go right up to the roof, but supported a gallery, reached by a spiral stairway in one corner. The actual kitchens were usually separate but adjacent buildings. Next came the body of the hall itself, being a long high room with a stamped earth floor covered by rushes. Furniture would have consisted of rough benches and tables. In early halls, warmth was provided by a fireplace in the middle of the floor, venting through a hole in the roof. This was later modified by the provision of a fireplace with chimney against one wall. Light was admitted through windows, usually only on the interior or bailey side. Glass was rare and expensive. Often only the upper part of the window was glazed, the lower part being secured by a shutter. At the far end of the hall was the dais, on which was the high table where the lord ate. He might have the dignity of a chair – hence our modern word chairman, signifying the person in charge.

Behind the dais, and likewise separated from it by a wooden screen, was the solar or great chamber. This was the lord's private apartment and contained his bed and his personal goods. It would probably have had a separate *garderobe* or latrine. In course of time, these quarters became divided up into suites of rooms – bowers for the ladies, withdrawing rooms and bed-chambers.

Ignoring the Hollywood treatment of baronial splendour, the first impression would have been one of smell – unwashed bodies, cooking, smoke and the filthy floor. Then there would have been the noise of men shouting and laughing, excited by drink; sweating serving men rushing in and out carrying platters laden with meat and pots of drink; dogs brawling on the floor, men picking quarrels and swearing mighty oaths. Above it all, the lord and his guests would preside. This was a small close-knit intimate society. Even the lowliest would see his lord daily, and some of the reflected glory might well rub off on the scullion and the cup-bearer. We are accustomed to the bare walls of castles today, but when inhabited, the rooms would have either been painted in bright colours, or hung with tapestries.

Of the domestic aspects of the castle, the next in importance to the hall was the chapel. Not all men and women were equal in the sight of God, and chapels were often two storey affairs, with the upper gallery reserved for the privileged. This would normally be accessible only from the great chamber, while the bulk of the troops and servants would worship below. Some chapels were small affairs, little more than oratories, while other castles had a parish church outside the walls. In other cases it became fashionable to establish collegiate churches within the precincts, complete with accommodation for the canons. The clergy, however, frequently served as the learned assistants of the lord, besides administering to the souls of his retinue. The chaplain kept the books and looked after the correspondence, as well as instructing the lord's children in the elements of learning.

The demise of the keep accentuated the move into separate internal buildings within the bailey. Those castles constructed around gatehouses featured the lord's apartments above the entrance passages. The problem there was that the portcullis machinery would have intruded into the living rooms – only the large multi-storeyed gatehouses can have proved a satisfactory solution.

In the larger castles at the end of the thirteenth century, the old community spirit was disappearing fast – with the advent of the mercenary garrison. The Norman castle was peopled by the owner and his sworn followers and servants. At Conway, the great hall is in the outer bailey, and was for the use of the troops. The kitchen was still a separate building on the other side of the courtyard. In the inner bailey was the king's hall and the king's apartments, and as his status demanded it, there was another room known as the presence chamber. Here, the king, or his deputy would hold court and dispense justice. On a smaller scale, at Bodiam, the rooms were built all around the quadrangle. One complete block houses the hall for the garrison, the servants' quarters and their kitchen. The other two thirds of the quadrangle are occupied by the owner's kitchen and buttery and his hall. Then comes the great chamber with the solar above it. Next was the ladies' bower and bedchamber, of which one can still see the fireplaces, the chapel and the steward's quarters. Firstly, the garrison is entirely set apart, and secondly, the kitchen communicates directly with the hall. This must have greatly improved the standard of the food.

The personnel of a castle varied greatly depending on its size and importance. Large garrisons were rare in peace-time anyway. In command was the *castellan*, either the owner or his deputy. In the case of one of the greater barons with several castles, most of them would be left in the care of a *castellan*. In the case of a royal castle, the commander was usually called the constable. Most barons would have a small group of knights, usually landless younger sons, as their personal retainers, who would live at their expense and eat at their table. They acted as bodyguard and companions, and might ultimately be rewarded with a land feoff – carrying with it an obligation for a period of castle duty. The responsibility for the security of various sections of the walls of the larger castles, was often a hereditary office of certain families. Thus the towers of many castles have family names.

Below the knights came the esquires, the apprentice warriors who were being trained. A knightly family might send one of their sons to be educated at the household of their feudal superior. There he would be instructed in weaponry, riding and in the code of conduct of his class. In addition, he would learn basic good manners, and perhaps be given some book knowledge by the chaplain. In return, he would be expected to serve as a page to the household, wait at high table, and perhaps look after the equipment of one of the knights or the lord himself.

Below the nobility came a group of soldiers commonly known as sergeants. They did on occasions fight on horseback, although not so heavily armoured as knights, but more usually formed the backbone of the infantry. Mostly they were freemen of the yeoman class, and could hold land by feudal tenure. The class distinctions among the infantry are difficult to define exactly, but it seems that crossbowmen ranked further down the scale than the sergeantry. These groups formed the backbone of the feudal army. In dire cases of emergency however, there was provision for raising the peasantry for defence of hearth and home. This was strictly a form of Home Guard, and would have been little more than a rabble armed with agricultural implements. Farming was far too important to have one's peasants tagging along on a campaign away from home.

In addition to the fighting men, a castle housed a number of specialists. Firstly there would be a group of paid overseers and officials, responsible for the administration of the lord's affairs. A castle was usually the centre of a farming operation, supervised by bailiffs. The reeve was the lord's man of business. He gathered in the various money dues from the tenants, and was probably the most unpopular man in the district. A baron grew wealthy on the labour of others. The peasants were obliged to work in his fields and grind their corn in his mill – for a percentage of the flour naturally. They had to plough his land with their oxen and provide their waggons to cart his supplies. They had to put up with his hounds riding all over their own crops, and suffer his pigeons to eat their grain. The lot of the villein, tied to the land and unable to move at will, was not a happy one.

A castle would also employ a number of tradesmen, from whose duties so many of our modern surnames originate. The steward was responsible for the conduct of the household, with a staff of cooks, gardeners and others, down to the lowest of the low, the scullions. Fletchers made arrows and coopers made barrels. Carpenters plied their trade around the place, and the smiths shoed the horses. The armourers cared for the war stores – a full-time job even in peace-time. Their supervisor would be the marshal, the official in charge of discipline among the garrison and responsible for its war readiness. Finally, there was the butler whose domain was the buttery – which had nothing to do with butter. The name comes from the French word *bouteille* – a bottle, and was the department concerned with the supplies of wine and beer, carefully stored by the cellarers.

From the foregoing, it can be seen that life within a castle was highly organised, and subject to a strict caste system. Those living there however, even the humblest, were often better off than those outside. They were never likely to go short of food and clothing, and had the advantage of belonging to a group with a certain *ésprit de corps*. Looking down from the lofty walls, they could afford to disdain the wretched civilians below.

Living in a castle meant extremes of discomfort – cold, damp and often rotten food. For those who knew nothing better, this probably did not matter much. Life was comparatively short, but in many ways lived to the full. For the rich there were certain compensations in the way of amusements, while for the poor, life was one unremitting round of toil, enlivened by the occasional feast.

When not at war, the upper classes spent much of their time preparing for it. Routine training included sword practice and tilting at the quintain. This was a shape of a figure suspended from a swivelling pole. Any off centre shot would cause it to swing round and clout the rider as he swept by. A good marshal would also see to it that his archers practised regularly at targets, and if he had a group of longbowmen, this was particularly important. A bored garrison was one likely to make trouble, so it was better to keep them occupied and out of mischief.

For the knights, there was the tournament – a form of mock battle fought over a considerable area of country. These took place from time to time, not only in this country, but abroad as well, with competitors coming from far afield. This was a valuable source of income for knights without a patrimony to inherit. The rules were fairly loose, although the aim was to unhorse rather than kill your opponent. The defeated knights forfeited their horses and armour to the victors. To stage such a show, one had to be extremely rich. A tournament could well last several days, during which the competitors had to be fed and housed in a style befitting their status. The whole affair was a splendid show, but could on occasions get out of hand – governments were frequently forced to ban them. Firstly because they caused a vast amount of damage to valuable agricultural land, and secondly because they were a sufficient excuse for a large number of fully armed men to gather together to plot rebellion. They had their useful moments however. At a tournament in Champagne, in 1199, many of the participants in the Fourth Crusade took the Cross.

The equipment that a knight could lose in such an encounter would represent several thousand pounds in today's money. His most valuable possession was his charger, without which, he was one of the common herd who fought on foot. In addition, he needed a palfrey for normal riding and a pack-horse to carry his armour and baggage. Anyone who has seen the Bayeux Tapestry knows what the Normans looked like. On their heads they wore conical metal helmets with extended nose-pieces. Their bodies were covered by long garments of chain mail, known as hauberks, underneath which they wore a leather jerkin to protect their skin from chafe. Personal weapons were the two-handed sword and the lance, the latter used at this early stage as a thrown spear. The thoroughbred horse able to charge at speed came in the twelfth century, while William's men would have trotted to the attack on ponies. Finally, the Norman knight had the familiar kite-shaped shield – without heraldic devices.

During the twelfth century, the hauberk was replaced by a shorter mail tunic, belted at the waist, with a head piece or coif, and without sleeves. During the early part of the thirteenth century the hauberk again became longer and fitted with sleeves. The head was covered by an enormous pot-shaped helmet, and mittens and leg coverings of mail were added. Around the middle of the century, secondary defences of plate armour began to be added to protect the joints and the shoulders. The helmet took on a more rounded form, to deflect blows, and the mittens were divided into separate fingers. After this, more and more pieces of plate were added, covering the legs completely. Also, the fashion for heraldic devices became general, being carried on the shield, the surcoat over the armour, and on the trappings of the warhorse. Complete plate armour came in at the beginning of the fifteenth century, but with the advent of the hand gun, declined into decadence. Suits of armour became reserved for ceremonial purposes, and monarchs were still portrayed in them right up to the end of the seventeenth century – wearing them with coronation robes and over silk stockings and knee-breeches.

An outfit of armour was one of the hallmarks of a knight – without it, he was a nobody. It was part of his duty to provide himself with the necessities of war in order to fulfil his obligations. The foot soldiers had to make do with leather jerkins for protection, which were however, reasonably proof against sword cuts.

In a society which had no form of packaged entertainment, food and drink loomed large among the things that helped to make life bearable. Men of all classes worked hard in the fresh air, and needed large quantities of food to keep themselves going. Feasting, although not an everyday event, was a most popular form of passing the long evenings. There are lists of the provisions consumed at some of the more famous gatherings – including such items as swans, peacocks and curlews that would be unacceptable today. Domestic animals were much smaller in the Middle Ages, as was the crop yield per acre. One of the main sources of meat however, was a direct product of the noble love of hunting, a pastime that was reserved strictly for the upper classes – the penalties for poaching were at times extremely severe. In addition, most castles would have had gardens and fruit trees, as well as fish ponds for the Friday and Lenten meals.

Many royal courts had already in the Middle Ages, established a reputation for sumptuousness and luxury. Frederick II is said to have lived in great style in his castles in Sicily, having imported many Moslem ideas. The growing trade from the East via Italy contrived to make the lot of the wealthy more and more pleasant throughout our period. There was a constant interchange among the castle dwellers of Europe, and the roads were crowded with travellers. Men mixed together on Crusades, or visited tournaments in different countries. Flemish mercenaries served in England, and English troops fought in Italy. The international scope of the church also fostered contact – there was even an English Pope at one time. Monks came and went within the houses of their Orders, and bishops were appointed to sees not necessarily in their own countries.

There was much beauty in the Middle Ages. The craftsmen who

produced Salisbury Cathedral and the stained glass at Chartres must have had a sense of mission – in the midst of the squalor and the cruelty, the beggars and the leering cripples, the disease and the brief life expectation. Existence in a castle could be depicted in some ways as idyllic – for the 'haves'. The 'have-nots', in spite of their perquisites, could not really be envied. Castles however, have a grim reputation that clings to them, which is in many ways justified. The owner of a castle, providing there was nobody strong enough to stop him, could do what he liked. He could use his position for the extortion of exorbitant dues, and not all members of the nobility were imbued with the spirit of chivalry. After the fall of the powerful Hohenstaufen emperors, the robber baron became a feature of German life – preying on travellers and his neighbours. In England too, during the anarchy of Stephen's reign, the breakdown of law and order was seized upon by certain elements as a licence to plunder. The *Anglo-Saxon Chronicle* gives a vivid account in the entry for 1137. It describes the tortures – 'They hung them up by their feet and smoked them with foul smoke . . . They tied knotted cords around their heads and twisted it until it entered the brain'. And so on in that vein, with the devices used becoming more and more unpleasant. The *Chronicle* also tells of the levying of protection money from the villagers, and when the inhabitants could not pay, their huts were burnt down. This sort of thing went on all over the place, not only during the twelfth century, but as late as the fifteenth, when English troops went on the rampage in France. During the Third Crusade, Richard I happily watched the execution of 2,700 Moslems all at one sitting. Mediaeval kings were not interested in humanitarian ideals when they tried to impose stable government. The fact was that an untroubled peasantry produced more and thus added to the royal income.

All castles had some form of prison, and anyone who had the misfortune to be thrown into it, could expect to be uncomfortable. The lord had control of local justice, but in fact, the death penalty was not so often inflicted as might be supposed. Any lord would prefer a money fine to a useless corpse dangling from the gallows. Torture was an accepted way of extracting information – and was to be so in many parts of Europe right up to the eighteenth century. The public visiting castles today expect something for their money in the way of horrific atmosphere but it is as well to remember that not every castle had an unenviable reputation like that, for example, of Berkeley, where Edward II was so foully murdered. Blinding and mutilation were acceptable punishments for crimes, and contemporary chroniclers did not clamour for leniency. Before condemning the cruelty of the Middle Ages, we have to first examine the record of the twentieth century in this respect. Castle overlords were probably no better or no worse than some of the products of modern totalitarian regimes, who likewise have practised oppression on a large scale. The difference is that the mediaeval peasant, with few exceptions, did not really long for freedom, as he did not know what it was, and would not have known what to do with it. The *Bauernkrieg* in Germany and the Peasants' Revolt in England were localized events, and did not seek to completely overturn the established order. The twentieth century however, has seen free nations crushed by conquering idealogical systems – bent on destroying their individuality and employing a system of economic exploitation. The gauleiter and the village commissar display remarkable similarities in character and performance to the petty lord in his castle.

PLATE DESCRIPTIONS

1. Castell St. Angelo, Rome.
Originally the drum-shaped middle part was the mausoleum of Hadrian, built in 135 AD. In the sixth century this was converted into a Papal stronghold, and served as such throughout the Middle Ages. Frequently attacked, little of the original work survives. In the early part of the sixteenth century, it was modernized through the addition of angle bastions – to form a citadel for the Vatican.

2. The Roman Walls of Portchester Castle, Hampshire.
Portchester was one of the Roman forts of the Saxon shore, built towards the end of the third century to ward off the attacks of Saxon pirates. In its original form it was simply a walled camp flanked by round towers, and was known as Portus Adurni. In the twelfth century the Normans built a castle in one corner of the Roman enceinte, including a magnificent rectangular keep. The plate shows a length of the Roman outer wall and ditch.

3. The Aurelian Wall, Rome.
This illustration shows a part of the Aurelian Wall, the original defences of Rome in ancient times. This was still in use in the Middle Ages when it was considerably modified by being raised and having a gallery added.

4. Loches, France. The Angevin donjon.
One of the oldest rectangular donjons in France, it formed part of the defence system around Tours. Unlike other donjons, the strip buttresses are rounded and very narrow. The castle was later improved by having an outer enceinte added with massive towers, which came to a salient point instead of being rounded.

5. Bramber Castle, Sussex.
This view shows the motte, typical in size and shape. Its interest lies in the fact that it is situated in the middle of the bailey, instead of at one corner. Bramber was one of the earliest Norman castles to be built in England, although little remains today after the destruction in the Civil

War. Just outside the gate of the castle is the original church which now serves the civilian community.

6. Castle near Lake Van in Turkey.

This view shows a castle in Turkey, probably of Crusader origin and built in the early thirteenth century. Although the design is French, the site could well be Germanic, perched as it is on a rocky promontory and almost impossible to approach.

7. The Tower of London. The White Tower.

The original keep of William the Conqueror's fortress built to overawe London. It is known that the construction was supervised by Gundulf, the Bishop of Rochester. Although much restored, the illustration shows the corner buttresses carried up to form towers – the roofs of which are later additions. Also, the small keep has disappeared. Note the battered plinth as a deterrent to the miner.

8. Restormel Castle, Cornwall.

This is the classic example of an English shell keep. This view shows the original motte with the encircling wall on top and the projecting chapel. Inside, the buildings were arranged around the ring wall, leaving a courtyard in the middle. As well as the chapel, one can still determine the position of the hall, the kitchen and the great chamber. The whole complex, surrounded by its ditch, formed a one-ward castle, without further baileys or other enclosures.

9. Lewes Castle, Sussex.

Another example of the shell keep, but flanked by towers. Originally, Lewes was one of the earliest castles built by the Normans to secure the South Coast and their communications with the Duchy. It featured two mottes, one of which is now covered by modern buildings.

10. Another view of Portchester Castle.

Originally a Roman shore fort, like Pevensey it had a Norman castle added to one corner. This plate clearly shows the rectangular keep, which is still in a fine state of preservation. This is surrounded by a later enceinte flanked by towers. To the left is the gatehouse and barbican.

11. Farnham Castle, Surrey.

The main castle of the Bishopric of Winchester. Originally a motte and bailey castle, Henry of Blois added a stone keep on top of the mound early in the reign of Stephen (c. 1138). After the accession of Henry II, the castle was slighted, but was probably rebuilt at the end of the twelfth century. The shell keep here enclosed the whole motte in masonry, as the bulge at the bottom of the wall indicates. Additionally, it was flanked by small rectangular towers, one of which can be seen in the illustration.

12. Rochester Castle, Kent.

One of the best known of the Anglo-Norman rectangular keeps. Note the small-keep with stairway and entrance. Also the increasing size of the window apertures as the height increases. The circular tower built after the siege of 1216 cannot be seen in this view. Some 25 metres (82 ft) high, it was built around 1128 by the then Archbishop of Canterbury, William of Corbeil, on earlier foundations of Bishop Gundulf.

13. Castle Rising, Norfolk.

A different type of rectangular keep, being lower in height and on a broader base. Situated in the middle of older earthworks, it presents a distinctly less martial impression than the more lofty keeps. Instead of the usual three, there was only one storey above the basement, although by subdividing some of the rooms at this stage, a partial second storey was formed. At the front is the chapel to the right, and the small keep or forebuilding to the left. The latter was originally timber roofed and had a gatehouse at the base. From here the stairs ascended through a second gatehouse and then through a third gate into the main building.

14. Norham Castle, Northumberland.

A further example of the rectangular keep. Built to defend a crossing of the Tweed in the mid twelfth century. Although ruined, it still gives an immense impression of power and strength.

15. Orford Castle, Suffolk.

The first of the 'experiments', Henry II built it between 1165 and 1173 to act as a counterweight to the ambitions of the Bigod family in the county. The plate shows the basically round keep with its buttressing flanking towers. In the foreground is the entrance via a forebuilding.

16. Avila, Spain.

This shows a section of the walls of Avila, one of the most noteworthy examples of military engineering in the eleventh century in Europe. Nearly two miles long, the walls included eighty-six towers and ten gates, and were built by Raimond of Burgundy from 1088–90. An Italian was said to be the designer, and such rounded towers did not appear elsewhere in Europe until the end of the twelfth century.

17. Dover Castle, Kent.

One of the last rectangular keeps to be built, started in 1180. This is enclosed by the almost contemporary inner enceinte, which still featured square flanking towers. Besieged in 1216 by the French, the outer enceinte was then added, featuring the rounded towers and the massive complex of the Constable's Gate. Many of the towers were cut down to mount artillery in the nineteenth century. The triangular work in the foreground is also a nineteenth century addition when the castle formed part of the defences of the area. Although featuring two enceintes, the castle is not truly concentric, as there was plenty of room for an attacker to concentrate between the walls.

18. Falaise, Normandy.

The rectangular keep was built by Henry I on the site of the castle that was the birthplace of William the Conqueror. After the fall of Normandy, Phillip Augustus added the round Talbot Tower, the machicolation of which was in its turn a later embellishment. Falaise was one of the Norman frontier castles, situated on the main road from Caen to Le Mans, and in an area fought over during the latter part of the Second World War.

19. s'Gravensteen, Ghent, Belgium.

The castle of the Counts of Flanders. Extensively restored in the late nineteenth century, the present work was begun in 1180, on the site of an earlier castle. In the centre is the keep, with a palace building to the left. The wall rising from the moat is flanked by small towers supported on the buttresses. In the foreground, the embrasures in the tower are covered by wooden shutters, common practice at the time.

20. Niort, France.

Built by Henry II Plantagenet in his Angevin dominions, this castle is unique. Although the vast bailey has disappeared, the interesting twin donjon has survived. In the illustration you can see the two towers joined by a curtain of almost the same height. In the foreground, the corner tower has a strongly battered base. The early attempt at machicolation can be seen on the inside wall of the far tower, supported by a single arch.

21. Vianden Castle, Luxembourg.

This is one of the largest castle complexes in Europe. Its origins go back some 1,000 years, and it features a hall that could accommodate 500 men. It was one of the royal residences of the Hohenstaufen dynasty, and from it comes the Orange-Nassau family, at various times the rulers of the Netherlands.

22. Krak des Chevaliers, Syria.

The greatest of the Crusader castles and certainly the best preserved of the larger ones. The illustration shows the natural strength of the site, and the various defensive levels. The present castle is mainly the work of the Hospitallers, carried out at the beginning of the thirteenth century, although there are some later Moslem additions. It finally fell only through trickery, after many months of abortive siege operations that had only penetrated the outer enceinte.

23. Sidon Castle, The Lebanon.
An interesting small Crusader work built beside the sea. Note the stone corbels to carry hoardings and the high entrance – also covered by a hoard or perhaps a stone brattice.

24. The Jerusalem citadel.
Again a mixture of Christian and Moslem work. Note the massive batter of the outer wall. The tower has an obvious Eastern style turret, and odd machicolation only on the corners.

25. Kokorin, Czechoslovakia.
A fine example of a now renovated fourteenth century stronghold in Central Bohemia. In the background is the massive keep with its strong machicolation and lack of apertures. To the left is the hall building which would have contained the main living quarters. Note that in the foreground the merlons are pierced with arrow loops.

26. Kerak in Moab, Jordan.
Although not showing much detail, this picture perhaps captures the surroundings and the atmosphere of the now ruined Crusader castles. Situated on a typical spur site, the castle was separated from the country by ditches hewn through the solid rock. It had two baileys, an upper and a lower, making it half concentric. It was already a fortress in Byzantine times, well before the Crusaders arrived on the scene, and they lost it to the Muslims as early as 1189.

27. Pernstejn Castle, Czechoslovakia.
Although the accommodation has been much modified, Pernstejn in South Moravia has retained several features that are typical of the central European castle. The tower to the left is the original non-residential keep which has been however, reduced in height. Note though, the bridge connexion from the main body of the work, which would have been the only entrance. All the window openings are high up, and turrets have been built out to give machicolated protection to the vulnerable corners.

28. Friars Castle, Spain.

This impressive ruin sited on a rocky hillside bare of cover, is typical of many Spanish works. Note how the tower has been grafted on to an outcrop of rock to give it an immensely solid foundation. The lack of cover and the stony ground would make the place extremely difficult to approach.

29. Angers, Loire.

This illustration gives a good impression of a stretch of the curtain flanked by the impressive towers, rising out of the solid rock. Note the flanking apertures fairly low down and able to cover the base of the wall. Built between 1228 and 1238 during the minority of St. Louis, the towers were cut down by Henry III during the Wars of Religion.

30. Aigues Mortes, France.

A view of the walls of the entrenched camp.

31. Aigues Mortes.

This illustration shows a section of the walls of the entrenched camp, laid out on Roman lines by Louis IX's son, Phillipe le Bel. Note the brattices over the door in the foreground and in the middle of each section of curtain.

32. Tour de Constance, Aigues Mortes.

Built as a royal residence at one corner of the entrenched camp from 1241 to 1250, as a preliminary to the crusade of Louis IX. The embrasure on the top is a later artillery modification. Although a residence, note the complete lack of windows.

33. Rosito Castle, Italy.

A small mediaeval castle with a keep that owes much to Norman example. On one side the rock plinth falls away steeply into a ravine, while on the other sides it is surmounted with a simple curtain. Note how the base of the plinth has been sculpted outwards both to deter mining and to deflect missiles.

34. Castel Nuovo, Naples.

This is one of the most impressive castles in the whole of Italy. Its very solidity proclaims its northern origins. The builder was Charles of Anjou, and work started in 1283. Between the two gate towers is a triumphal arch erected for Alphonso I in 1470. The towers are all machicolated, and the enceinte has been surrounded by a second and extremely low girdle of walls – similar to Harlech and Beaumaris.

35. Castel del Monte, Apulia.
Frederick II's hunting castle. The illustration clearly shows the symmetrical shape and the wonderfully clean design. One can also see the doorway with its mixture of classical and Gothic architecture.

36. Knepp Castle, Sussex.
This view shows the motte, surmounted by the ruins of a later keep.

37. Bramber Castle, Sussex.
A view of the ruins of the gatehouse keep, a victim of the Civil War. Bramber originally featured a motte in the middle of the bailey, and was one of the earliest castles in England after the conquest in 1066. The original wooden gateway was later replaced by a masonry structure.

38. Pevensey Castle, Sussex.
The interior stairway leading to the chapel.

39. Pevensey Castle.
This plate shows the remains of the Roman walls of the shore fort in the background. In the foreground is the Norman castle – a fine round flanking tower of the outer enceinte. Note the berm between the wall and the ditch, and the sally port to the right of the tower.

40. Framlingham Castle, Suffolk.
The stronghold of the Bigod family, rebuilt in stone at the beginning of the thirteenth century. This picture shows the gate and the typical rectangular towers.

41. The Muiderslot, Netherlands.
Sited at the southern end of the Ijssel Meer, in the vicinity are a number of nineteenth century gun batteries. This castle has been beautifully restored, but is hardly a tough defensive proposition when compared with the contemporary Welsh castles. It is built of brick, and the residence is sited against the far wall, leaving a bailey in the middle. The gatehouse is not particularly prominent.

42. Carcassonne, France.
This picture clearly shows the concentric arrangement of the two lines of walls, one above the other. Note that the merlons are pierced with arrow slits. The restoration started in 1844 and was entrusted to Viollet le Duc, who made a magnificent job of it – in spite of some criticism. As it now stands it is probably more or less as the Black Prince saw it in 1355 – he withdrew without attacking. Inside the town but abutting on to the walls is the castle of the Trencavels, forming a citadel – it is separated from the town by a ditch and barbican.

43. Lewes Castle, Sussex.
This view shows the barbican, with the original Norman gateway in the background. This was connected by short walls to the newer gatehouse built at the end of the thirteenth century. This was defended by a machicolated parapet over the gateway, which was closed off by a portcullis. The corner towers are corbelled out from the straight walls.

44. Carcassonne.
This view shows the Porte Narbonnaise with its barbican. Many of the towers had their own cisterns and kitchens, thus forming independent strongholds.

45. Carcassonne.
Another view of the outer enceinte.

46. Amberley Castle, Sussex.
Built *c.* 1379 by the Bishop of Chichester, and used as a fortified residence. This view shows the gatehouse, typical for the late fourteenth century with its towers flanking a simple entrance. The castle was sited to control a ferry over the river Arun, and is now in private ownership.

47. Rhuddlan Castle, Wales.
Work started in 1277, and it was one of the early castles built by Edward I. The inner bailey, which is basically what we see here in its ruined state, was trapezoid in plan with drum towers at the two most salient corners. The other two corners had flanked gatehouses. The outer enceinte was however, irregular in shape and not particularly strong. As the distance between the two defence lines was in places up to 70 metres (228 ft), it can hardly be described as concentric.

48. The Tower of London.
A fine example of a concentric castle. Although overbuilt by later constructions, one can still follow the course of the exactly parallel double wall system. The original keep sits uselessly in the middle of the later defences.

49. Boulogne, France.
This plate shows the Porte Gargoyle, and is included to illustrate the type of gatehouse that was developing in the thirteenth century, flanked by massive drum towers.

50. Conway Castle, Wales.
Partly built up on a solid rock base, the castle rises above the town which was founded at the same time. Note the massive spur at the base of the tower in the centre of the curtain. The railway bridge needless to say, is

an example of fake Gothic, but tones in well with the castle. Conway was built to overawe a defeated people, which it probably succeeded in doing with such an impressive skyline.

51. Caerphilly Castle, Wales.
One of the most spectacular non-royal castles in the British Isles. This view shows the platform or outer enceinte and one of the great keep-gatehouses. It was more or less impregnable except to amphibious assault. The present ruinous state is a result of slighting during the Civil War – the effect of a few barrels of gunpowder.

52. Harlech Castle, Wales.
The first of the Edwardian concentric castles. The illustration shows the low outer ward dominated by the curtains and towers of the inner. The gatehouse at the front with its twin flanking towers is typical for the development of this feature at the end of the thirteenth century.

53. Beaumaris Castle, Wales.
The most perfect concentric castle ever built. This aerial view shows the plan perfectly. Note that the gatehouse in the foreground was never finished. Unlike Harlech, the outer enceinte also has small flanking towers.

54. Caernarvon Castle, Wales.
This is a detail illustration of a postern gate. The recess around the lintel would originally have housed the bridge in the raised position. Note on the right the small turret in the angle of the wall with an arrow-slit to flank the doorway. Such posterns could be used by the garrison to sally out to attack a besieging force, and if the blockade was not too efficient, to bring in supplies and messages. They also offered a chance to escape if all else failed.

55. Caernarvon Castle, Wales.
This is a good illustration of a part of the enceinte. Here one can clearly see the arrangement of flanking towers and the wall-walk. Note that below the wall-walk there is an enclosed gallery with arrow slits, in the thickness of the wall itself. Each tower overlooks the adjoining portions of the parapet.

56. Kidwelly Castle, Wales.
This was basically a D-shaped work. The plate shows the straight side with the projecting chapel, the corners of which are protected by spurs. A private castle, it was started around 1275, and like some of the Edwardian works, was part of a walled township. To the left of the

picture, the gatehouse can be seen.

57. Caernarvon Castle, Wales.

A more detailed plate showing the Eagle Tower. The turret theme was used both here and at Conway. Note that the merlons are pierced for arrows. At the base of the tower is a water gate or postern.

58. Goodrich Castle, Welsh border.

Another of the marcher or frontier strongholds on the Welsh border. Inside is a rectangular keep that is completely dwarfed by the later outer enceinte. Note the truly massive spurs at the base of the towers, while the whole work is built up on a rock base – a formidable obstacle to the miners' picks.

59. Bodiam Castle, Sussex.

Arguably the most beautiful of all English castles. Built from the profits of the 100 Years War, it rises from the centre of an artificial lake, joined to the land originally by two causeways. This view shows the southern or water gate, with its machicolated tower. Although the interior was generously laid out, in view of French raids, Bodiam was built to be defended.

60. Lucens Castle, Switzerland.

Another typical western European castle, only this time the *Burgfried* is round and situated at one end. Note that there is no real enceinte as in an English or French castle – the buildings with their outer walls form the defences with a hillside below.

61. Spiez Castle, Switzerland.

Situated near Lake Thun, it is a twelfth century town castle. It has the typical Germanic non-residential keep tower in the middle, around which are grouped the main buildings.

62. Burg Stahleck, Rhineland.

A typical Rhine castle, situated above Bacharach. Built by one of the local nobility when the Emperor, Frederick Barbarossa was absent on business in Italy. The owner used it as a base for warfare against the local bishops, but it is now a Youth Hostel. Again there is the roofed allure and the central keep tower.

63. Marienberg Castle, Wuerzburg, Germany.

This is a detail illustration to show the ditch flanking of a typical German castle of the late twelfth century. The towers are much slimmer, although well provided by arrow loops. The conical roofs are also typical. Note that the curtain is roofed and instead of crenellations, there are loops pierced through at intervals.

64. Kenilworth Castle, Warwickshire.

This castle like neighbouring Warwick was transformed into a palatial residence at the same time. This illustration shows however, the keep which was retained. The corner buttresses are more prominent than usual in rectangular keeps and form quite solid towers. Note however, the complete absence of flanking arrow loops.

65. Manorbier Castle, Wales.

An excellent illustration of Manorbier Castle in West Wales clearly showing the interior layout.

66. Warwick Castle and the River Avon.

This shows the late fourteenth century Caesar's Tower and the palace building. The new forward enceinte at Warwick was probably the last serious attempt at building a strong defensive feature in an English castle. The palace however, was a sign of the times.

67. The Vicar's Pele, Corbridge, Northumberland.

Probably the smallest and least spectacular of the Pele towers, this served as a place of refuge simply for the local priest in times of danger. The corner brattice machicolation was not there for decoration however – there was a serious defensive intent. Such a tower would have been capable of resisting a small band of robbers bent on quick plunder.

68. Herstmonceaux Castle, Sussex. The main gate.

Here, the defensive element is only for show. The gatehouse is machicolated and well provided with arrow loops, but the windows on either side would have been a more inviting target for the missiles of an attacker. The situation however, is very beautiful, and the designer succeeded in making the place look like a castle.

69. Oravsky Podzamok, Czechoslovakia.

This is a good illustration of a castle built in 1267 in Central Slovakia that has utilized to the full the natural defensive structure of the site. It would be almost impervious to the traditional methods of attack. The river Orava forms a natural protective barrier, and the hill, besides being steep, would be impossible to mine. Such a castle would provide a secure refuge from all but the most determined attackers.

70. Villeneuve-les-Avignon, France.

This plate shows the Fort St. André, built to watch the Popes. Built 1362 to 1368, the building gives an impression of massive strength. Made purely for military purposes, it foreshadowed the later artillery fort. Note that the towers are on the same level as the curtain to give a continuous fighting platform. At the corner on the right is an elaborate latrine.

71. The Papal Palace, Avignon.

This particular illustration gives perhaps the best view of the fortress nature of the complex. This is not by any means a comprehensive design like say Beaumaris. It grew up over a number of years in the early part of the fourteenth century. Although defendable, it also had to house the entire papal court, and thus needed representative rooms. One can see however, the arched machicolation that appeared at Niort and Gaillard.

72, 73. Beaucaire Castle, Rhône, France.

This castle has a triangular donjon, built by Raymond VI, Count of Toulouse at the beginning of the thirteenth century. The machicolation is of later date. This plate gives a good impression of the wall-walk from the inside, supported on corbels. Beaucaire was the scene of that most beautiful of all mediaeval romances, *Aucassin and Nicolette*.

74. Tarascon, France.

Directly opposite Beaucaire lies Tarascon, a royal castle dating from around 1400. Again, there is a level fighting platform and all-round machicolation frieze. Although the exterior is forbidding, the inside features generous rooms, and in the middle is a courtyard used for plays and jousts.

75. Villeneuve les Avignon.

Situated on the opposite bank of the Rhône to the Papal palace, this plate features the Tower of Phillip le Bel – originally built to keep an eye on the Pope over the river. The machicolation was added in the fourteenth century. Note the latrine built out from the wall.

76. Fougères, Brittany.

One of the castles along the old frontier with France. Built on natural rock, it dates from the thirteenth to the fifteenth century and has thirteen towers. It was last taken by storm at the end of the eighteenth century – during the revolt in the Vendée.

77. Vitré, Brittany.

Another of the Breton frontier castles. The work is partly concentric, and the illustration shows the two enceintes clearly, in many ways similar to Carcassonne. Below the crenellations can be seen the putlog holes for inserting the supports for the hoarding.

78. Château de l'Hers, France.

The still impressive remains of a once powerful castle. The building has been designed to blend in perfectly with the terrain, and on such a rock foundation would be impossible to undermine. On top of the tower can be seen the supports for a machicolation frieze.

79. Josselin, Brittany.
One of the main castles of the Rohan family. Although the river façade looks formidable, note that the parapet has disappeared. The main building is a fine early Renaissance construction. Five of the original nine towers were demolished by order of Richelieu in the seventeenth century.

80. Saumur, Loire.
The present building was erected at the end of the fourteenth century by Louis I, Duke of Anjou. The interior was completely remodelled in the fifteenth century. Saumur is an example of the French castle turning into a fine comfortable residence.

81–87. Bonaguil Castle, France.
This series has been included to show various details of castle construction.

> **81.** A sally port well recessed within the walls.
> **82.** An ornate fireplace.
> **83.** The loophole from a flanking chamber right in the base of a tower. This could adequately protect the base of the wall.
> **84.** Stairway leading up to a tower. Note the recessed lintel to house a raised bridge and the loophole above the door – probably for a hand-gun.
> **85.** The interior of a firing position.
> **86.** A postern viewed from the outside. Note the recess for the bridge and the slot above for the counterpoise beam.
> **87.** Gateway from the inside – one for pedestrians and the other for carts and horses. There is a firing position on each side.

88. Azay-le-Rideau, Loire.
Built between 1518 and 1529 for the financier Gilles Berthelot – a commoner. The architecture is Gothic and the building is purely a residence, but turrets and machicolation have lingered on to create an impression.

89. Bonaguil Castle, France.
This was one of the last real castles built in France, and dates from 1482–1530. It was thus well into the artillery period. Here we can see the prow-shaped machicolated donjon and the double entrance gate. The

interior was traditional, but outside there were low platforms for mounting guns.

90. Donnington Castle, Berkshire.

All that remains after the siege in the Civil War, is the ruined gatehouse. In 1644 it held out for three months against a force of some 3,000 Parliamentary troops, only to fall in 1646, right at the end of the war. The castle however, was greatly strengthened by modern earthworks.

91. Salses Castle, Roussillon, France.

This is a transitional work, built at the end of the fifteenth century by a Spanish engineer. Although it was a square with corner drum towers and a powerful keep, the whole complex was sunk deep into its ditch. Not much of the work can be seen from the distance. The defences were all designed with artillery in mind, as can be seen in the curved walls to deflect shot.

92. Consuegra Castle, Granada, Spain.

Like most of the large Spanish castles, this one is late in period (fifteenth century) and dates from the wars between the king and the nobility. Note the natural glacis bare of cover and the two lines of walls before the interior is reached. In this case, the inspiration was probably French, judging by the shape of the towers.

93. Penafiel Castle, Spain.

Although comparatively late (fifteenth, early sixteenth century), Penafiel still retains the donjon combined with a powerful enceinte. The masonry has been sculpted into the rocky base. Note that the parapets above the machicolation have been pierced for hand-guns.

94. La Calahorra Castle, Spain.

This design is nearer to the French rectangular castle with corner towers. There is no keep and the domed turrets are unique. Note that the outer enceinte has a layer of gun-ports below the crenellated parapet, and that the tower bases have been well scarped. The whole building is far less decorative than many Spanish works.

95. Valencia Castle, Spain.

This is another example of the keep-based castle. This is reminiscent of a Norman keep fitted with rounded buttresses and transported into fifteenth century Spain. The towers have no loopholes and are far too slender to have served any really useful purpose.

96. Fuensalda Castle, Spain.

Another variant of the keep castle, built in 1500. Again, the towers have no flanking capability for the keep, but the smaller ones around the enceinte have loop-holes. The effect is rather like a mini-Vincennes which is heightened by the fact that the entrance to the keep is high up and can be isolated by a bridge.

97. Orgaz Castle, Spain.

A small but neat work in a mixture of styles. Contrast the Moorish square tower with the rounded French one and note the lack of low-level flanking positions. It is odd that the small hanging turret at the corner is the only part to feature machicolation.

98. Mendoza Tower, Spain.

This work again is a combination of keep and enceinte. The tower was traditional in Spain, but the roof is a modern addition. In this case, the outer enceinte is primitive and the protection of the gate is inadequate. The only provision for defending the base of the tower consists of the small brattices which may well have functioned as latrines in an emergency.

99. Manzaneres el Real, Madrid Province, Spain.

This is a fine example of an ornate Spanish work. It dates from 1435 and has a distinct French flavour about the design. It is concentric, and has masked firing positions below the parapet. The harshness of the land-scape is a great contrast to the majority of north European castles.

100. La Mota Castle, Spain.

Situated at Medina del Campo, this fine work is another example of the Spanish tower and bailey castle, dating from the fifteenth century. It also features a close outer enceinte to make it a concentric castle. The masonry work is of a high standard and the whole complex has been well preserved.

101. Rothenburg ob der Tauber, Germany.

Rothenburg is famous rightly for its well preserved walls. This plate however shows the so-called Toepplerschloesschen – a German pele tower. Toeppler was the Burgermeister of the town. He built this tower at the end of the fourteenth century as a refuge, not far outside the walls. Originally it was surrounded by a wet ditch.

102. Heidelberg Castle, Germany.

This represents a mixture of styles, with again little from the Middle Ages remaining. The main residence of the Electors Palatine, it had Gothic, Renaissance and Baroque wings. The ruin that we see today is a result of the sacking by troops of Louis XIV in 1689. Although basically a palace, its ruinous state lends it an air of strength.

103. Pfalz, Rhine.

This was a toll collecting station, built on an island in the Rhine, opposite the town of Kaub. It was built for the Archbishop of Trier in the early fourteenth century on an ashlar base in the shape of a ship. Contemporary prints show Blücher's army crossing here in January 1814.

104. Wolframs Eschenbach, Bavaria.

A typical German barbican erected in front of an older town gatehouse leaving a confined courtyard between the two. The parapet has gun loops, and around the arch can be seen the squared-off recess for the drawbridge. The town is famous as being the birthplace of Wolfram von Eschenbach, the creator of the romance Parsival.

105. Langeais Château, Loire.

One of the earlier châteaux to be built in the Loire Valley, replacing a much earlier mediaeval castle. Although palatial inside, the exterior has retained many basic defensive features. The open defensive parapet has disappeared, to be replaced by a continuous machicolated gallery. The gateway is still protected by a counterpoise drawbridge, the supports of which fit into the slots above the portal.

106. Amberg, Bavaria.

This plate shows the inside of another town gate barbican. Note the permanent *coursière* over the wall-walk and the oblong slits for crossbows or hand guns.

107. Festung Marienberg, Wuerzburg, Bavaria.

This plate is included to show the development of a castle into a baroque fortress. Little remains of the original work except for the thirteenth century round *Burgfried*. On top of the hill is the princely residence mostly built at the end of the sixteenth century. The seventeenth century bastions can be seen descending the hill on either side – they enclose the whole area of the castle itself, and the fortress remained active until 1867.

108. Inoux Castle, Pyrenees.

A fine illustration of a mountain stronghold. The design is in many ways Moorish with its squared off angles. On such a site there was no need for a complicated enceinte – the only way to approach it would be via the village and up the side of the spur.

109. Windsor Castle, Berkshire, England.

This view shows the shell keep with its early nineteenth century additions by Wyatt. Although a fake – only the first level is genuine – it looks somehow right, especially as it dominates the silhouette of the castle.

110. Montagnana, Italy.
Work was in progress here from the thirteenth century through to the fourteenth century. The town is enclosed in walls with a perimeter of one mile. The illustration shows a section of these walls together with part of the Castello di S. Zeno, which acted as a citadel. The flanking towers were polygonal.

111. Senigallia Rocca, Italy.
An artillery fort built, *c.* 1480. Note how the profile has been lowered, although the walls still retain their splayed base. Also, the traditional machicolation and crenellation has been retained, an indication that infantry defence was still thought of as being based on the parapet.

112. The Rocca at Ostia, Italy.
This was one of the earliest artillery forts to be built. It is included here on account of the mediaeval features that still cling to the design. In the narrow flank of the bastion you can see the embrasure of a casemated gun, while the whole parapet is crenellated and machicolated.

113. Arundel Castle, Sussex.
This view shows the much restored eastern face. Of the original castle, only the shell keep on the motte remains. The rest was largely destroyed after a siege in the Civil War, and was rebuilt at the end of the nineteenth century by the 15th Duke of Norfolk. It is still the residence of the family.

114. The Rocca at Forli, Italy.
Another example of a late mediaeval Italian artillery fort. Built in the 1480's, the towers and walls form a continuous platform. Note the embrasures for flanking the ditch, as well as the machicolation. Forli also retained the traditional keep.

115. Sirmione, Italy.
Situated on Lake Garda, the style is florid in the extreme. From the solid simplicity of the Hohenstaufen works in the south of the country, the later Italian castles went to the other extreme. Small wonder that so many of them were battered down by the artillery train of Charles VIII of France in the campaign of 1494. Built in the fifteenth century, its high silhouette reminds one of a Victorian toy fort.

116. Konopiste Castle, central Czechoslovakia.
In spite of the baroque gateway and the large windows, this castle has retained its defensive aspect. Note the powerful keep with the enclosed

machicolated gallery and the spurs at the base. This is flanked by another equally solid tower with the original hall in between. The building to the left and the tower are probably later additions.

117. Haute-Koenigsbourg, Alsace.
This fine mediaeval castle was destroyed by the Swedes during the Thirty Years War. The ruin was restored on the orders of Kaiser Wilhelm II, during the German occupation of Alsace-Lorraine. A mixture of Gothic and Renaissance, most of the work was done during the early part of the twentieth century.

118. Stolzenfels Castle, on the Rhine.
Bought as a ruin by Frederick William IV of Prussia, it was totally rebuilt in neo-Gothic in the nineteenth century. There was no attempt here to restore the original – it was simply turned into an imaginative country residence.

119. Castell Coch, near Cardiff, Wales.
The restoration of this small castle was commissioned by the Marquess of Bute in 1875. The result was most praiseworthy, with few trappings of fake mediaevalism. Only the roofs of the towers have come in for some criticism, owing to their typically French aspect.

120. Liechtenstein Castle.
A well restored example of a typical Germanic castle. The buildings on a spur site cluster around the old *Burgfried*, in this case, a cylindrical tower.

121. Neuschwanstein Castle, Bavaria.
Surely the classic nineteenth century re-creation, begun in 1869 for Ludwig II, King of Bavaria. The exterior is pure fantasy, while the interior is richly decorated with mainly Wagnerian themes. Ludwig only spent some hundred days in the place, and it was there that he was told of his deposition in 1886. Three days later he died in the Starnberger See, in mysterious circumstances – his buildings had almost bankrupted the state. This castle is popular with film makers and advertising agents.

GLOSSARY OF
TECHNICAL TERMS

Allure   Archère

ALLURE The wall-walk behind the battlements.

ARCHÈRE A loop-hole.

BAILEY The courtyard of a castle. Also known as a WARD.

BALLISTA A projectile-throwing engine worked by tension.

BARBICAN An advanced work to protect a gateway.

BARMKIN Border word for BAILEY – used only in connexion with pele towers.

BARTIZAN A turret projecting from the top of a wall or tower.

BASTIDE The name for certain military settlements laid out on Roman lines in southern France in the fourteenth century.

BELFRY *(Beffroi)*. A siege tower.

BERM Ledge at the base of a wall to stop debris falling into a wet ditch.

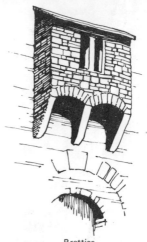

Bartizan   Brattice

BRATTICE (*Bretèche*). This word is confusing. Some authorities use it to denote a hoarding *(q.v.)*. Others use it to mean an open floored latrine as a machicolation over a gate, for example. Viollet le Duc employs it to describe a temporary wooden structure to defend the end of a bridge.

BURGH An Anglo-Saxon fortified township.

CASEMATE Gallery built outside the base of a wall. Fitted with loop-holes for archers to fire in the face of attackers. Also used for a vaulted chamber in the base of a tower from which flanking fire could be directed.

CASTELLAN The commander of a castle. Also CONSTABLE.

CAT A popular name for a PENTHOUSE, a moveable shelter for miners and rams. Also known at times as a SOW or MOUSE.

CHEMISE A wall built closely around a donjon.

COUNTER-CASTLE A castle erected by besiegers to protect their operations.

COURSIÈRE Wooden roofing erected over a wall-walk.

CRENELLE The gap between the merlons on a parapet or battlement.

CURTAIN *(Courtine)*. The correct name for a length of wall.

DONJON French word for keep. Not to be confused with dungeon. *Burgfried* in German and *Mastio* in Italian.

ENCEINTE The full circuit of walls and towers around a fortified place.

ESCALADE The assault of a castle by climbing its walls.

ESCHAUGETTE See BARTIZAN.

FAUSSE BRAYE A line of defences on the floor of the ditch at the base of the walls.

GARDEROBE Latrine.

HOARD/HOARDING Wooden gallery projecting from the parapet to enable defenders to see base of wall and to drop things on those below.

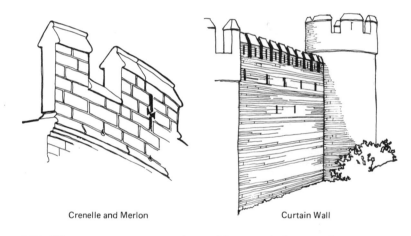

Crenelle and Merlon   Curtain Wall

KEEP The strongest part or place of last resort in a castle.

LIST Interval between two lines of concentric walls.

MACHICOLATION Permanent stone version of hoarding.

MANGONEL Throwing engine worked by torsion.

MANTLET Mobile protective screen used by besiegers as cover.

MERLON The solid part of parapet between two crenelles.

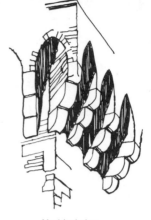

Hoarding and Coursière

Machicolation

MEURTRIÈRE Hole over a passageway for dropping things on those below.

MOTTE Steep artificial or natural mound of earth.

PALISADE A fence of wooden stakes.

PARAPET Protective screen of crenelles *(q.v.)* and merlons *(q.v.)* on top of a wall or tower. Generally referred to as battlements.

POSTERN Small exit gate or sallyport.

RAVELIN A triangular shaped outwork sited in the ditch in front of a curtain.

SOLAR Private room for lord or his family.

TALUS Sloping wall thicker at base.

TRÉBUCHET Siege engine worked by counterpoise.

VICE Spiral stairway in thickness of wall.

BIBLIOGRAPHY

The following works should all be available through public libraries, or made available by special request, and many of them contain much fuller reading lists.

Anderson, W. F. D., *Castles of Europe from Charlemagne to the Renaissance*, Elek, London, 1970.

Barton, S., *Castles in Britain*, Lyle, Worthing, 1973.

Brown, R. A., *English Mediaeval Castles*, Batsford, London, 1954.

Clark, G. T., *Mediaeval Military Architecture in England*, Wyman, London, 1884 (2 vols).

Cruden, S., *The Scottish Castle*, Nelson, London, 1963.

Douglas-Simpson, W., *Castles in England and Wales*, Batsford, London, 1959.

Dutton, R., *The Châteaux of France*, Batsford, London, 1957.

Evans, H. A., *The Castles of England and Wales*, Methuen, London, 1912.

Fedden, H. R., & Thompson, J., *Crusader Castles*, John Murray, London, 1957.

Hindley, G., *The Castles of Europe*, Hamlyn, Feltham, 1968.

Hogg, I. V., *Fortress*, Macdonald and Jane's, London, 1976.

Hughes, J. Q., *Military Architecture*, Hugh Evelyn, London, 1974.

Leask, H. G., *Irish Castles*, Dundalk, 1946.

Oman, Sir Charles, *The Art of War in the Middle Ages*, Methuen, London, 1898.

Castles, Methuen, London, 1926.

Painter, S., *William Marshal*, The John Hopkins Press, New York, 1933.

Renn, D. F., *Norman Castles*, Baker, London, 1968.

Thompson, A. H., *Military Architecture in England during the Middle Ages*, Cambridge University Press, 1912.

Toy, W., *The Castles of Great Britain*, Heinemann, London, 1953.

The History of Fortification from 3000 BC to 1700 AD, Heinemann, London, 1955.

Tuulse, A., *Castles of the Western World*, Thames and Hudson, London, 1958.

In addition:

The excellent series of guides to individual castles published by the Department of the Environment.

The books in the series 'The Buildings of England' by Nicholas Pevsner, Penguin, Various dates.

INDEX

Figures in bold type refer to colour illustrations.